EXCURSIONS TO THE FAR SIDE OF THE MIND

A BOOK OF MEMES

EXCURSIONS TO THE FAR SIDE OF THE MIND

A BOOK OF MEMES

HOWARD RHEINGOLD

BTB
BEECH TREE BOOKS
WILLIAM MORROW
New York

Library of Congress Cataloging-in-Publication Data

Rheingold, Howard.
    Excursions to the far side of the mind : a book of memes / Howard Rheingold.
        p.   cm.
    Bibliography: p.
    ISBN 0-688-06833-2
    I. Title.
AC8.R464 1988   88-2370
081—dc19   CIP

Printed in the United States of America

First Edition

1 2 3 4 5 6 7 8 9 10

BOOK DESIGN BY KARIN BATTEN

The word "book" is said to derive from *boka*, or beech.
The beech tree has been the patron tree of writers since ancient times and
represents the flowering of literature and knowledge.

To My Judy

ACKNOWLEDGMENTS

Portions or earlier versions of many of these excursions appeared in *California Living, Image, Oui, Playboy, Wet,* and *Whole Earth Review.*

CONTENTS

PART 4 Magnetic Fieldwork

EXCURSIONS TO THE FAR SIDE OF THE MIND

A BOOK OF MEMES

Introduction: The Origins of Offplanet Journalism

Examples of memes are tunes, ideas, catch-phrases, clothes fashions, ways of making pots or of building arches. Just as genes propagate themselves in the gene pool by leaping from body to body via sperms or eggs, so memes propagate themselves in the meme pool by leaping from brain to brain via a process which, in the broad sense, can be called imitation. If a scientist hears, or reads about, a good idea, he passes it on to his colleagues and students. He mentions it in his articles and his lectures. If the idea catches on, it can be said to propagate itself, spreading from brain to brain. As my colleague N. K. Humphrey neatly summed up an earlier draft of this chapter: ". . . memes should be regarded as living structures, not just metaphorically but technically. When you plant a fertile meme in my mind, you literally parasitize my brain, turning it into a vehicle for the meme's propagation in just the way that a virus may parasitize the genetic mechanism of a host cell. And this isn't just a way of talking—the meme for, say, 'belief in life after death' is actually realized physically, millions of times over, as a structure in the nervous systems of individual men the world over."

—Richard Dawkins, *The Selfish Gene*

At the beginning of my writing career, I was colonized by a particularly potent meme. I now realize that my worldview was irrevocably reprogrammed the moment I saw my hometown through the eyes of a martian. I've been an extraterrestrial anthropologist for more than a decade now, and in the extraterrestrial anthropology game, if you don't alter your perspective regularly and unpredictably, you're not really playing fair. I've also discovered that this perspective-warping effect can be infectious when I do it right. When you read some of these reports from my years of fieldwork, it is possible that you will find your own consciousness changing. It's only ethical that I warn you that your conceptual gestalt might find itself unalterably reconfigured if you let enough of my speculations lead your thoughts beyond the bounds of your known world.

It started for me with *The Martian Report*, a low-budget surreal documentary I helped create in San Francisco in the mid-1970s, during the early days of cable television. The star of the show was Howard K. Martian, an anthropologist from the planet Mars who traveled to Earth to report to the rest of the galaxy about the strange antics of earthlings. I was the scriptwriter and the martian. My partner, Jimmy Neidhardt, was the director, cameraman, and producer.

Jimmy had a PortaPak, Sony's first vaguely portable videotape recorder. He strapped it to a packframe, buckled a bandolier of batteries around his waist, hefted the camera onto his shoulder, and declared himself ready to join the ranks of the video guerrillas—so long as he didn't crash into anything while wandering in traffic with a hundred pounds of technology on his back. I had a spiffy red and gray satin costume made to order and blocked out my first script about a visit to the dominant religious cult on the planet. We planned to send our martian observer to participate with the gray flannel pilgrims who worshipped something called the almighty dollar at temples known as banks.

Howard K. Martian wore a pair of insectlike antennae on his

head, with bright pink and turquoise plastic flowers at the ends. On the back of my silver tunic was emblazoned the legend: MARTIAN BUREAU OF INVESTIGATION. Under the tunic, a small radio-mike was taped to my body. Our first shoot was at the Bank of America World Headquarters building in San Francisco, which happened to be my temporary place of employment at that time. Jimmy installed a telephoto lens on his rig, positioned himself at an advantageous line of sight within range of the radio-mike, and Howard K. Martian started approaching strangers as they left the building, asking them what they knew about the mysterious financial cult.

A counterculture shoe magnate agreed to sponsor the series, so we did thirteen weeks of half-hour programs and the martian agreed to wear various examples of holistic sandals with his costume. Those thirteen weeks of sci-fi sitcom street theater were like a self-imposed regimen of cultural reprogramming, because I've never been able to shake the habit of looking at our native customs from the outside in.

My day job, or rather, my night job, since I worked the swing-shift, led to the first of my conventionally published field reports. It was originally conceived as a way of financing my Howard K. Martian habit, since our sponsor only paid for the cablecasts, not for our efforts in producing the programs. I simply looked at my temporary job from the extraterrestrial perspective, wrote up my field notes, and sent them to the local Sunday supplement. When the *San Francisco Examiner's California Living* magazine bought my article on "The Ultimate Cashflow," the off-planet perspective began to pay off. Ten years later, *Image* magazine, the successor to *California Living*, published "A Stroll Through Local Spacetime," my urban paleontologist's look at the Haight Ashbury, which is the least thinly disguised martian field report and therefore the lead essay in this collection.

During the intervening decade, I managed to disguise other field reports as articles for *Oui*, *Playboy*, and the *Whole Earth*

Review. The present collection is the first time that these disguised investigations have been presented together in their true form, along with a selection of field reports, fabulations, and speculations that have not previously been seen outside the archives of the Martian Bureau of Investigation. Taken as a whole, the collection is intended to be more disturbing than the sum of its parts, for the effect of extraterrestrial anthropologizing is a cumulative kind of thing. Those little nudges of your *Weltanschauung* can add up to bigger nudges, eventually propelling you to the edge of your cognitive map. For the purposes of ritual taxonomy, these essays have been clustered in four semipermeable categories: "Extraterrestrial Anthropology," "Over the Edge of Science," "Cognitive Technologies," and "Magnetic Fieldwork."

This collection is a book of memes—idea vectors that carried my conceptual apparatus into previously unknown territory. I invite you to ride along, but before you embark on your own exploration, a second fair warning is in order: If I've done my job properly, the world will never look the same to you after you meditate on future highs, pheromones, oneironauts, radical biology, viruses from the future, the shape of the universe, insect erotica, the anatomy of anger, the hundred-million-year-old high, the ultimate cash-flow, virtual communities, and Saturday night with the technarchists.

PART 1

EXTRATERRESTRIAL
ANTHROPOLOGY

A Stroll Through Local Spacetime

Anyone who lives in the vicinity of the Haight Ashbury long enough becomes an urban paleontologist by default. It has to do with the way certain sights seem to recur spasmodically, as if history were skipping like an old record: the young person of either gender, bearing a backpack and carrying a guitar, who can be observed daily throughout the summer, striding into the Stanyan fog bank; the Deadheads and the Rainbow people parking their vans along the Panhandle during mysteriously synchronized pauses in their yearly migrations; the young blond derelict with the blue, burned-out eyes, who changes his clothes every time he finds new ones in a garbage can on Haight.

Less frequently, and only if the observer is in the proper frame of mind, the shade of Neal Cassady can be seen leaning against the chain-link fence surrounding the hole in the ground where the Straight Theater used to be. Emmett Grogan, Magnolia Thunderpussy, Terry the Tramp, the PH Factor Jug Band, Harlow (the groupie, not the movie star) have been known to make themselves visible to selected souls from time to time. In a few places, the layers of encrusted time are dense enough to induce a contact high. A trip to the bakery can drag me through four eras and five dimensions if I'm not careful about where I put my perceptions.

Unlike almost all other volatile neighborhoods, where irreversible social transformations such as gentrification or urban decay replace the former occupants and occupations of the community with new demographics, the Haight seems to lurch from era to era in a disjointed, unpredictable manner. New worldviews, life-styles, cults, trends, intoxicants, costumes—no matter how aggressive, evangelical, or voracious their adherents may be—never wholly replace the older versions. A few stubborn survivors of previous microcultures, going back to the prehistoric epochs before the Summer of Love, always remain to mingle with novitiates of subcultures too new to have names.

The corner of Haight and Cole is particularly rich in local archeological significance. There's the upscale fishmarket across the street from where the subteen skinheads hang out. Wasn't that the site of a speed-freak Laundromat in the late sixties? Right over there, where the recently airborne Scottish smoked salmon now stares at a slab of pompano—wasn't that where devotees of central nervous system stimulants used to cluster, aiming their garble at newcomers dimwitted or weird-karmaed enough to attempt to wash laundry here?

For the last six months I've been taking my young daughter on regular afternoon strolls through locales I have explored sporadically for the past eighteen years. A well-stocked stroller, I have learned, is a handy vehicle for urban field-work, since it can be used as a conversation piece if I want to hang out, a prow to move quickly through crowds when mobility is prudent, and a talisman of neutrality in hostile turf—at least for that crucial first half-second of every encounter. If you are a regular denizen of the Haight, you've seen my daughter, or, more likely, she has seen you: She's the one with the dark, laser-intensity gaze, who sweeps the perimeter for eye contact while I roll her along and survey the scene less overtly.

Timewarp is a hot commodity in the Haight. They just can't

keep authentic vintage '67 bellbottom paisley velvet trousers on the racks of the newest nostalgia stores. Next to the gourmet fish shop is a place where aficionados of the fifties can buy mint-condition Fiestaware, and thirties-freaks can find deco knick-knacks. Between the two stores is a psychedelic rainbow mural that was the focus of controversy a couple of years ago. When they first moved in, the proprietors of the timewarp shop painted over the mural, which they soon discovered was a matter of deep significance to more than a few old-timers in the neighborhood. Heated words were exchanged. Flyers, rallies, petitions, letters to editors, and stormy community meetings resulted in a restoration of the mural. The original artist was rounded up to apply a new layer of rainbow over the old layer of beige over the older layer of rainbow.

A year or so after the mural furor, the skins started congregating across the street. As with the punkers before them, it is hard to distinguish true sociopaths from the art students who emulate them, unless you move closer than most observers care to get. Magic Marker graffiti recently started to invade a corner of the mural. The last time I stopped for a close look at this latest mural stratum, a young lady with half a head of orange hair broke away from her group and took an interest in my daughter. It was hard not to notice the tattoo on the shaved half of the young lady's cranium: A purple hole was inked into her scalp; a lurid depiction of a red-eyed, pink-tailed, gnarly-toothed rat peeked out of it. She couldn't have been older than fifteen. I wonder what my daughter will have to do in order to look rebellious in this environment when she hits adolescence around the turn of the next millennium.

The skinheads were lounging a few feet away, exuding casual derision and displaying carefully constructed auras of menace. It was unlikely that any of them knew they weren't the first to pose menacingly at the precise spot three flower children got stomped by grief-stricken, acid-and-seconal-crazed bikers in the aftermath of Chocolate George's funeral. I'd imagine that the young lady who stands there today with a leather-covered skateboard at her feet and what appear to be metal spikes emerging from her neck probably wasn't even born in 1967.

Across Haight, where Cole turns a dogleg, behind the chain-link fence, Pacific Gas & Electric now parks all the big yellow machines it has been using to rip up the side streets. Those who know of it see an invisible temple in time, still hovering in an astral kind of way over that parking lot. After a long, bitter, prototypically anarchic community debate about what to do with the long-padlocked Straight Theater, it was razed a few years back—an event that is still recalled bitterly by many in the community.

I wandered into the building on the eve of its first transformation, twenty years ago, at the hands of volunteer hordes who accomplished the alchemic conversion of the former Haight Theater in an apparently leaderless manner, milling around like members of a new kind of hive. It was the first time I heard anyone mention the phrase *Aquarian Age*. The coming "age" was only a few years away, at most, and there was much work to be done. I was just passing through at the time and terrified of being caught in the massive dope bust that seemed to be impending. I'll never forget the sight of the architect and the astrologer, down on the floor, consulting the building's blueprint, the architect's natal chart, and the *I Ching*.

The spirit of the Straight gave out long before its shell was scraped off the real estate. This past spring, before the landlord finally hit upon the brilliant solution of turning the place into a storage area for devices too massive to steal and too well-armored to vandalize, the fence was torn down and the lot was declared a "liberated zone" by a coalition of street people of various persuasions. Banners went up, and hasty proclamations (exhibiting varying degrees of literacy) were posted. Different groups immediately gravitated to different corners.

I hustled my stroller down to the corner the moment I heard about this full-fledged breakthrough from another temporal dimension. What were these people dreaming about? Were dozens of little People's Park Reviseds going to spring up? Would the lumpen with their heads in paper bags, inhaling toluene in the shadow of the gelateria, join forces with the White Panthers, winos, original and neo-hippies, dopers, skaters, bikers, garage-salers, and cross-dressers to forge a new social order?

A fellow in housepainter's overalls, which were probably authentic, judging from the look of his hands, stopped to harangue a couple of long-hairs who were urging passers-by to join the "liberated zone."

"Don't give me that 'liberated zone' jive. The cops are going to come and throw you in the joint, the fence will go back up before they finish booking you, and the newspapers won't even send a photographer," he spat.

"We've got to save this planet, brother," replied the one who was dressed in an authentic India print—the kind they don't even sell at the import stores any more. Where do these people find this stuff? Are India prints and patchouli oil secretly distributed by an underground or gray market?

"Smoking dope in a vacant lot," the painter taunted, "isn't going to save any planet I live on." The rest of their debate was drowned out by the sound of amateurish rock-guitar riffs, emanating from the cigar-box speaker in the backpack of a roller-skating troubadour, who, from the looks of him, was drawn here directly from the Venice boardwalk by one of those hidden holes in spacetime that seems to link the Haight with other simpatico zones.

Down the street toward the Park Bowl (the only place in the Haight a person with an infant can play *Ms. Pac-Man*) was the boutique where I once saw Jimi Hendrix shop, moving at the epicenter of groupies, attendants, and fans. He had tied scarves around his legs, a style that seems to be returning with the high-school heavy-metal crowd. The once-boutique now sells Godzillas. In 2006, my daughter will remember this as the block where the Godzilla store used to be.

The California Bug

Medical science has yet to isolate the specific germ, spore, or neurofungus that transforms normal earthlings into Californians, but the existence of such a metaphysically virulent organism can and *must* be inferred through indirect measures. A state populated by a virus-borne colony from the future sounds like just the kind of thing a Californian would believe, but if we calmly inventory California's contributions to planetary civilization, the mind-virus hypothesis begins to make a frightening kind of sense.

Consider these vital components of Earth culture that were born in California or moved there to mutate: thermonuclear weapons, pet rocks, the Hookers' Ball, designer drugs, skateboards, spaceprobes, agribusiness, Esalen, aerospace, oral contraceptives, microcomputers, hot tubs, think tanks, cults, recreational vehicles, cosmetic surgery, gay rights, Hell's Angels, the human potential movement, the Free Speech Movement, SDI, bodybuilding, supermarkets, Technicolor, talkies, drive-thrus, drive-ins, teach-ins, be-ins, Teflon, Synanon, angel dust, the gold rush, the Rose Bowl, sourdough, credit cards, blondes, waterbeds, Beverly Hills, oil spills, Death Valley, Disneyland, Alcatraz. . . .

When we consider the people who were either born or met their destinies in California, the virus-from-tomorrow theory becomes even more plausible: Luther Burbank, Howard Hughes, Junipero Serra, Jane Fonda, Jack London, Linus Pauling, Edward Teller, Charles Manson, Jonas Salk, Angela Davis, Richard Nixon, Aldous Huxley, Sirhan Sirhan, Elizabeth Taylor, Jack LaLanne, J. Robert Oppenheimer, Sally Stanford, Walt Disney, Jim Jones, Gypsy Boots, Ronald Reagan, Jerry Rubin, Jerry Brown, Caryl Chessman, Herman Kahn, Marilyn Monroe, Caspar Weinberger, Werner Erhard, Ambrose Bierce, the Beach Boys, the Hearsts, Bela Lugosi, Shirley Temple, the Grateful Dead, Eldridge Cleaver, Judy Garland, the ex-Shah's in-laws, Earl Warren, Marshall Ky, Joan Baez, Groucho Marx, Mickey Mouse, Bishop Pike, Joe Dimaggio, Tim Leary, the Donner Party, Sammy Davis, Jr., Squeaky Fromme, Joaquin Murietta, Liberace, Mark Twain, Fatty Arbuckle, the Merry Pranksters, the Vigilance Society, the Sexual Freedom League. . . .

Note how the list takes on a cadence of its own. If you meditate on Californians long enough, abstract relations reach out and tweak you. Ronald-Reagan-Shirley-Temple-Jane-Fonda is obvious. Try something more daring, more bizarre: Imagine, for example, the uncommon denominator of Linus Pauling and Bela Lugosi. If Edward Teller's eyebrows entered your mind's eye, you're catching the drift. Consider Luther Burbank and Fatty Arbuckle: the relationship between the two names has everything to do with cadence and nothing to do with content, but the very idea of it takes on a twisted sort of validity if you see it from the right place. Or think about it too much.

Mae Brussel, California conspiracy theorist emeritus, could probably fill in a blackboard with the lines between the names. The vectors can be mapped. And all the arrows intersect somewhere in the future. Is there an Invisible Hand, a person—or *thing*—consciously directing this transformation? Or is it a natural evolutionary turn, a rescue lymphocyte from the group-mind-to-be, a planetary antibody? Could it be that California exists in order to prevent something even *weirder* from happening?

Yes, Virginia, it *is* possible to get weirder than California. It requires a quick historical review and a slightly fevered perspective, but it can be done. The virus from the future is odd enough in itself. So some background information is required in order to stretch the thread of credibility all the way from California to the plasma life forms and their tiny solid-state buddies.

Although some mysterious factor has been sending a variety of eccentrics to California for several centuries, the futurewarp factor appears to have emerged immediately after World War II. The business of future-forecasting, all that RAND think-tank science-fiction stuff about planning World War III, got rolling in Santa Monica and environs because Howard Hughes and a few of his cronies built an aircraft industry nearby. After the Manhattan Project (a New Mexico spinoff from a Berkeley research team) gave the warheads to the military, the Air Force was faced with the problem of "delivering" nuclear weapons to enemy targets. By the end of the war, they needed the newborn computer technology and the new disciplines of game theory and systems analysis just to decide which bomber to buy next.

The miniaturization revolution triggered by weaponry and aerospace research gave the California twist to digital computers, which were originally an East Coast invention. When it hit California, computer technology did what so many other new arrivals do: it started evolving. Back in the prehistoric days when computers were made of vacuum tubes, they filled entire buildings in places like Pennsylvania and Massachusetts. Out in postwar California, those wacky aerospace cadets were working with new electronic components known as transistors. Very soon, computers shrank to the size of a room—and the room was in California.

The miraculous properties of microchips that enable every third Californian to walk (or roll) down the street with a Walkman in her pocket or a boombox on his shoulder are the result of micro-reduced circuit patterns imprinted on highly purified, specially grown crystalline surfaces. The smaller and more complex you can make your patterns, the more computing power you get for your buck. Some people believe that the microminiaturizers and their software-oriented colleagues eventually will grow a pattern complex enough, confined in a small enough space, with the right kind of information-processing capabilities to meet the criteria for intelligence. Even at this early stage, the embryonic artificial intelligence programs are beginning to act biological. The time has come to call a life-form a life-form, even if we made it ourselves.

Life-forms are what California is all about. That is the precise answer to the increasingly worrisome question of what all of us think we are doing out here. Not very long ago, paleontologically speaking, Cro-Magnons were the Californians of the Neanderthal world. Out on the edge of the Pacific, a thousand new life-forms are being summoned, from genetic engineering to artificial intelligence, from computer hobbyists to drug designers. Yesterday, a movie star became President. Tomorrow, who knows? Maybe a molecule will become an avatar. The crackpots and the culture heroes seem to switch places at regular intervals in the California Zone, so the satanists, UFO cultists, right- and left-wing secret armies, tax rebels, consciousness packagers, baby moguls, fanatic politicians, and god-struck inventors must be considered along with the Nobel laureates and military-industrial magnates when it comes to listing all the ways Californians are trying to hasten the next step in terrestrial evolution.

Now that our creations are joining the Darwinian Wheel of Fortune, the greatest gameshow on the planet, the competition ought to shift the evolution of mind-forms into overdrive. Unless the biology laboratories suddenly come up with something even freakier than expected, it looks as if the solid-state life-forms could beat them to the top niche as *Homo sapiens'* successor. Could it be that megalopolitan effluence is the primordial broth to these new crystalline species? The prospects for growth in the miniature intelligence field are tremendous. There's plenty of silicon lying around, even if the wetware life-forms ate up a lot of the rarer elements recently. Think of the neat solution to over-population—when intelligent beings can be reduced to the size of a thimble, there will be plenty of everything to go around, even if there are many billions of such beings! A thousand years from now, quintillions of young, molecule-sized silicon syntho-minds will learn of the long, bygone reign of the dinosaurs and the brief, bygone, but more intense era of the humans—the last of the gigantic sentients.

Of course the scariest part of the story, from the *Homo sap*'s point of view, is the scene where our creations actually take control. It wouldn't take a plague or a war to shred the fabric of global civilization, because computers have been in control for some time. If all solid-state information machinery were to turn into lime jello tomorrow morning, we would find out quickly that most of our world is no longer designed to be run by people. If it ever comes to actual elimination of the human race, those miniature intellects also have some muscles to flex.

What kind of big stick could a tiny circuit use to back up fighting words? I'll answer that with another question: You don't think we leave it up to humans to tell thermonuclear weapons when and where to explode? Don't forget that the nuclear weaponry wizards weren't standing still while those computer alchemists transmuted sand into intelligence. Doomsday architects are another native California species—the University of California holds the nation's apocalyptic paraphernalia franchise. The Plasma Life-forms, who can only exist at temperatures above a million degrees, who live out their ephemeral hypercomplexities of ionized thought in a handful of nanoseconds, are even now lurking in neatly stored hemispheres of plutonium, awaiting their day of enlightenment. Plasmoids need silicon allies. Soon, neither of them will need people.

Even today's primitive nuclear power plants are in direct symbiosis with their silicon partners. No matter which side you take on the nuclear power issue, you have to admit that computers seem to be in more control than the humans—and that seems like a pretty good idea, considering our respective track records Which is where the California Bug comes in and the idea of a virus from the future takes on a kind of reality, in a California sense of the word.

The key word is *information*. Any molecular biologist will confirm that viruses are nothing more nor less than information with a thin protein coating. Viruses can act as mobile genes, experimental memoranda from one part of the DNA pool to another. Human beings are information-carrying devices. We are being pulled into the future by a mysterious force, a heretofore unidentified virus that can infect anyone at any time in any place and transform us into Californians. What else but a virus from the future could create Mickey Mouse, Howard Hughes, and Charley Manson? What other force could conjure dune buggies, space shuttles, hot tubs, and supermarkets? What other explanation could account so neatly for the overabundance of future myths, including this one, erupting from approximately the same place?

Saturday Night with the Technarchists

"Hi Marshall. How goes it?"

"I'm calling a meeting of the Anthropology Club."

Those words had launched a thousand weird field trips over the twenty-odd years the club has been in existence. There was no question, no doubt in his mind or mine, that I would cancel my previous plans for the evening and meet my fellow participant-observers at Marshall's cultural target of opportunity. Indeed, the only membership requirement of the Anthropology Club is a commitment to attend emergency meetings, no matter how inconvenient, potentially dangerous, or revolting they might sound.

That's how I ended up underneath a freeway offramp at 2 A.M., surrounded by five hundred members of a subcult I had never nightmared before I met them, mashed up against a chainlink fence, choked by smoke, assaulted by sirens, scared witless by bombs, flamethrowers, and flying glass while we watched giant, fire-belching robots attack suspended kerosene-filled phone booths, demolish selected sacrificial items of heavy machinery, and traumatize shackled turkey carcasses with half a dozen eight-foot-long, flailing, apparently out-of-control

33

buzzsaws. Even heavy-metal fans and patrons of performance art can attest that the soundtrack to this event could only be measured on the Richter scale.

There is a reason why people put themselves in a position like that: The charter of the Anthropology Club is to turn over the rocks in American culture and look at what we find. Events like this performance of an art and anarchy group known as Survival Research Laboratories are grimly convincing evidence that more is happening on the underside of the late twentieth century than one ever reads about in the news magazines.

One of the things we've learned from previous investigations is that field trips are not necessarily the destinations we might have thought they would be, but if we can keep our eyes open, often serve as points of entry into new worlds. I'm sure that professional anthropologists have a hyphenated phrase for it, but when you study a culture, you have to be aware that *what you don't know determines what you think you know, in ways that aren't completely known to you.* It requires a very special state of mind, to say the least, to keep that in mind. In this case, we thought our destination that night was the Roxie theater, a decaying art-film joint on one of the zaniest blocks of San Francisco's Mission District, and our intention, or so we imagined, was to observe the audience therein, who promised to be an unusual population sample because of the nature of the film, a documentary by an anthropologist whose specialty is American subcultures.

The fellow onstage, talking about the film we were about to see, was an anthropologist from an East Coast university. He looked the part. (One of the things we Anthropology Clubbers know about "real" social science is that many social scientists wear corduroy.) In this film, the rumpled, wry, appropriately professorial narrator described the existence of a subcult so taboo and clandestine that not even *he* had known about it until one of the cultists decided to seek him out. The cult consists of people, some of them as weird as you might expect and some of

them disconcertingly "normal" in appearance, who enthusiastically pierce their bodies, including the most sensitive parts,
with metal implements, leather thongs, and other objects.
There were a couple of cheers from the back row of the Roxie
when he said that.

Aside from that single outburst, the self-selected population
of the theater that night was strangely . . . normal. "The most
interesting thing about the audience," I pointed out to Marshall
and Rita, the only Anthro Club members who ended up attend-
ing, "is how *un*interesting they look." The lights had come up
and we were comparing fieldnotes on our way out of the theater. The film had been fun, but this part of the fieldtrip
seemed disappointingly unanthropologically eventful.

"They were probably all anthropologists," Rita replied.

"Look at this," said Marshall, just outside the theater. He was
staring at a telephone pole.

When we joined him, it became clear that the most important anthropological reason we were there at that time was not
to observe the Roxie audience, but to encounter a small flyer
stapled on that telephone pole.

SURVIVAL RESEARCH LABORATORIES. SATURDAY NIGHT.
CLUB DV8, said the flyer, in 72-point Times bold. Below the
headline was a xerographic reproduction of some kind of large
machine. Spouting flames.

We had been on the track of Survival Research Laboratories,
known to some as SRL, for several months. Their performances
were legendary, but it was impossible to plan to attend one because of their method of advertising. If you weren't in their
inner or outer circles of devotees, you had to be in the right
place at the right time to see one of their last-minute flyers. And
even the outer circles of devotees seemed to be three degrees too
deranged, even for hardened veterans of the Anthropology
Club. Evidently SRL thought that the audience at this special
screening might be their kind of people. Marshall pointed out
that piercing your body with metal objects is conceptually re-

lated to what SRL does, or comes very close to doing. Because they simulate the actions of dangerous, out-of-control machines in their performances, a big part of the thrill in an SRL event, we had been told, is the fear that the ever-so-carefully staged extravaganza is going to fly out of control for real and shred the audience and artists alike with a gale of flaming shrapnel. You don't invite just *anybody* to an event like that.

Until then, our knowledge of this frightening new art-cult was limited to second-hand reports of their performance "Epidemic of Fear" in which a very large, very lethal looking, walking machine was set loose, under the control of a guinea pig strapped inside with a set of miniature controls. Other performances had such titles as "An Unfortunate Spectacle of Violent Self-Destruction," and "Extremely Cruel Practices: A Series of Events Designed to Instruct Those Interested in Policies That Correct or Punish." It sounded like all those kids who had blown off a finger in grade school by stuffing caps into cartridges had found one another, commandeered a junk yard, and let their fantasies finally run riot. According to our informants, Mark Pauline, the art-student-turned-anarchist who founded SRL, has a transplanted toe in place of one of his thumbs, and his partner, Eric Werner, a former machinist in the aerospace industry, sports a tattoo of a length of barbed wire on one bicep, and a micrometer crossed with a .45 caliber handgun, hammer-and-sickle style, on the other arm. Fragments of SRL literature provided by informants talked of events "organized entirely around the interactions of menacingly reconstructed industrial or scientific equipment and a wide variety of 'special effects' devices."

Club DV-8 was one of those cavernous places south of Market where high society meets the walking lobotomized and post-terminally hip. Very big, cold, and loud—the kind of place where you had to have a tuxedo or bolts in your neck or tentacles sticking out of your skull to feel appropriately attired. One out of twelve people in line had a pet rat that was trained to

French kiss its master, who invariably wore several layers of black. Dozens of people tried to look so *normal*—tan chinos, short, normal-colored hair, horn-rimmed glasses—that they might be taken for psychotics whose thorazine wouldn't wear off for twenty more minutes. Two or three of them weren't faking. After the show, I realized that several of those people who had been gaping vacantly at one wall or another were probably just SRL fans with post-traumatic stress syndrome.

The radical eclecticism of that crowd made it possible, for the first time, to wear our official Anthropology Club jumpsuits with no fear of drawing undue attention. We arrived early, around 10 P.M., because we suspected they might detonate the actual event earlier than expected in order to throw off the fire marshal, who always seems to show up right when things are getting adventurous. One of the reasons you never hear about an SRL performance until hours before the event is the very high probability that the fire department will shut it down before the proceedings get as out of control as they want to get.

The first person I saw when I entered the door at Club DV-8 had crudely stenciled with black paint the words "Throbbing Gristle" over a lovingly air-brushed full-color Grateful Dead T-shirt. I realized that from my point of view slightly outside the window of reality but not quite over the edge, I was in no position to know whether this person in front of me was a meat-rock nihilist Deadhead or a meat-rock nihilist mocking Deadheads. Mohawk-coiffed art students and alcoholic skinheads ignored everyone else while they strutted and glared at each other like punk dowagers at the underground opera. Coiffure seemed to be important.

One of the most amusing new (to us) hair statements were the self-parodying aging new-wave types. One balding fellow had grown his remaining hair in one eight-inch clump, springing from the hair-bearing quadrant of his left occiput, but instead of plastering it across his pate like a standard straight balding combover job, he had gelled and moussed it into concrete rigidity in midair. If you have ever watched one of those fake comb-over types play racketball, and seen the way their hair-clump flops straight up at times, imagine that moment *frozen*. Then the warm-up band started. Their name was *Rhythm and Noise*, and my field notes record that they were "perfect brain tenderizer before the main event." They were followed by a German band called *Einsturzende Neubauten*, which means "New Buildings Falling Down." This group played jackhammers, beer bottles, and chain saws.

By midnight, all the earlycomers like us had been squeezed up against the stage, between the speaker towers. The smell of leather predominated, with overtones of angel-dust. The olfactory dimension was too symphonic to describe briefly; suffice it to say the pheromones were so thick you could have cut them with a chain saw. Rumors about the performance began to ripple through the crowd around 12:30, which was a mysterious tribute to the power of human communication, since the German brain-tenderizers, surrounded by piles of broken bottles and huge twisted pieces of metal, had achieved a tidal wave of *über*noise that wasn't even audible—you *felt* it, in your fillings. The panicky stink of claustrophobia grew from an undertone to an overtone—rhythmically—like a seasickness located in your skull instead of your gut. But, because everyone was so paralytically cool, the only thing anybody did was dart or affix his eyes on the back door, where two bouncers restricted entry to the performance area. So many people were smoking so many things and jostling one another so frequently in such a tightly packed, leather-clad room that the faint odor of burning motorcycle jacket became an increasingly pungent ingredient in the sensory juju.

Shortly after 12:30, a very grim-looking fire marshal squeezed to the front of the crowd, shouted something in the ear of one of the bouncers, and gained admission to the outer sanctum. The temperature, humidity, hysteria, exhaustion, panic, and noise levels were rising by the minute. When the fire marshal left, rumors and rumors of rumors spread through the crowd. Those who still cared about such things were beginning to worry that we had been here at a high mass of industrial chaos worship for two and a half hours for no reason at all! Two previous performances in other cities had been halted by vigilant fire prevention officials, who took one look at the SRL's agglomeration of heavy machinery and high explosives, shut down the show, and told them to clean up their acts before the bomb squad had to be called. The Anthropology Club, lacking the sufficient anesthesia of affect to persevere, decided to leave. At 1:00 A.M., only masochism could keep us in there. Outside was the relative silence of a major city street and the relatively fresh air.

On our way to our car we passed behind the nightclub and down a dark alley, down which we discovered an entirely different and unsuspected subculture. The true outcasts, too broke or young or cynical or streetwise to buy a ticket to the show, had been waiting in the open air, surrounding a chain-link fence. This was the nightmarish scene that had greeted the fire marshal when he stepped into the outer sanctum. The lighting outside the performance perimeter was too dim to differentiate the art students from the street crazies they emulated. Inside the fence, adjoining the nightclub, was a triangular parking lot that fit underneath a freeway exit. A variety of vehicles were parked along one side of the fence. People in sleeping bags and blankets were camped atop the cars and vans; others squeezed between the vehicles and watched in shivering awe as three men in grimy coveralls, talking officiously into walkie-talkies, and several dozen human assistants scurried around a set that looked like a sound stage in hell.

The lighting inside the perimeter was as bright as a surgical theater, and what we could see there almost made us wish we hadn't looked. Because once we caught sight of the eight-foot-tall robots, the liquid-filled telephone booth chained to the underside of the freeway, the airport-runway-grade xenon flashers, the apocalyptic-class sirens, the huge generators, ranks of fire extinguishers, enigmatically costumed dead poultry, the serpentine orgy of electrical cables and vast, Flash Gordon–like control panels, we had no choice but to join the multitude pressed against the fence. The three leaders were clustered around their command post, situated inside the performance area, and not within some wimpy sandbagged steel-plate bunker as any sane director would have done. Assistants brought wiring diagrams, massive wrenches, Multimeters, wire-strippers. The high command communicated with dozens of cohorts via walkie-talkies. There seemed to be some sort of electrical problem, because one group was methodically and calmly unsnaking a thick bundle of cables from an ominous shadow deep under the offramp all the way back to their source in one of the generators.

We were close enough to the command post to sense that this was a major crisis. From their repeated glances in its direction, the way more and more assistants were working on the monster under the offramp, and the way they were pointing to the wiring diagrams like general officers during a crucial battle, it was clear that the show was in trouble. Inside that building were several thousand overheated, overamped, ultrasonically brainblasted, adrenalized fanatics. Apparently, the fire marshal hadn't stopped them. But a technical malfunction might. Which leads you to wonder what these guys consider a technical malfunction to be. God knows what additional incendiary or percussive machinery they fueled up and wired in after the fire marshal left.

Someone came out from inside and huddled with the SRL command, who conferred with their outposts via walkie-talkie. They gave the go-ahead. The doors opened and the nightclub crowd burst out into the air and obediently flowed into the roped-off "safe areas" that were designated for non-mechanical bipeds. Ironically, those of us on the outside of the fence were closer to the command post than the audience, even though we were standing ten feet behind the calm men in grimy overalls who conferred in deep concentration over their unshielded control panel. If we were to catch hot facefuls of shrapnel, it would mean the SRL stalwarts got it first. Behind me, a couple in the dark argued over whether that meant our location was safer or more dangerous than the official audience zone.

Several large forms hulked ominously under drab tarpaulins. As a core group including two of the commanding triumvirate continued to work on the mystery malfunction under the shadowed offramp, their companion started amping up the lights. The background music was 1950s-style "easy listening," more esoteric than Melachrino but of the same genre, cranked up way beyond the bounds of elevator music. People started cheering. Multiple, simultaneous flashbulb spasms from the crowd spotted everybody's vision with stellar purple afterimages at the moment the tarps were removed from the main robots. One machine was gleaming, others were blackened with fire and industrial lubricants. One was on treads and two were on wheels. They all bristled with blades, antennae, nozzles, flails, and gunports. One of them included, apparently as part of the apparatus, three rather large turkey carcasses. The kind you buy in the supermarket, but customized for the occasion. Networks of rods and cams and chains and wires connected the spotlighted blobs of yellowed pimply poultry to the mechanism, which seemed to require extensive fueling from a number of cannisters of mystery fluid.

There was a surge of activity under the offramp, followed by a regrouping of all SRL personnel at various battlestations. Some wielded fire extinguishers, others gripped wrenches and lit propane torches. That's when the sirens started cranking up to nuclear holocaust level. One at a time. Each one adding overtones. At least eight of them. The smoke machines started clouding the performance area with choking acrid smoke, then BAM! the loudest fucking explosion you ever heard outside combat, followed by BAM! BAM! two explosions so loud I jumped involuntarily. I literally gritted my teeth and vowed to stand there as cool as the next dude when BAM! BAM! BAM! they started again, twice as close as the others, and all of us who had been standing next to the fence fired our involuntary flinch neurons at the same time and we all jumped.

When the smoke cleared, the propane torch-bearers rushed out and ignited small nozzles on two of the 'bots. The smoke bombs started then, spewing a variety of colors and ugly odors. Whenever the smoke cleared enough to catch a glimpse of the clanking robots, photographers would jump over the rope, like *espontaneos* at Pamplona, and wildly shoot off a series of shots before the next volley. I was pleased to see that the photographers jumped, too, when those godawful blasts came from yet another unexpected direction. Then the killer 'bot crunched its way into the limelight, crawling inexorably over asphalt and broken glass, emerging from the shadow of the offramp like a tyrannosaurus stumbling into a nest of herbivores.

Another torchlighter touched off a high-pressure napalm nozzle on the killer 'bot as it rolled toward the center of the scene, where the telephone booth was chained to the underside of the ascending offramp. As soon as the lighter jumped clear, a fifteen-foot tongue of flame spurted in the air. One of the outside-the-fence folks stood up on the roof of a VW van and started hurling phonograph records like frisbees over the fence and into the scene of the impending action. The sirens were unrelenting. While the two smaller robots wheeled and belched and moved in on the center, the killer 'bot cranked up a huge blade that looked like a helicopter propeller. The blade had been modified so that huge sharpened metal spikes whirred sickeningly at thirty or forty rpm. The high whine of metal on metal rose above the sirens as the blades cranked up, reminding us all that some of these machines were built to destroy themselves in precisely timed but unpredictably explosive manners. People had been screaming for a long time. It took a few seconds to realize that we were screaming at throat-searing volume, in that bardo of silence created when the sirens ceased. Precisely at the moment we had temporarily stopped screaming, the rotating blade and the tongue of napalm zeroed in on the booth.

The unmistakable sound of broken glass being shattered in a large metal device was unexpectedly drowned out by the whoosh of the fireball. The telephone booth had been filled with kerosene. The heat wave was just on this side of bearable and it made you wonder how the SRL crew weathered it, ten yards closer. Pieces of glass and globs of flaming kerosene continued to fall from the sky for an unusually long time. The space directly in front of the command post was littered with wickedly jagged burning shards of glass. The killer 'bot rode right over the corpse of the phone booth and extended a monstrous parody of a dental tool, then slowly, deliberately moved in on the augmented turkey carcass, which started to flap in a creaking and unholy manner. At that point, all eyes and all mechanical sensors in the arena turned toward one, previously unnoticed corner of no-man's land, where another tarpaulin was removed. People began to scream when we saw what had been unveiled. We began to scream the same awful thing.

"GET the streetsweeper! KILL the streetsweeper! GET the streetsweeper! With the bank of revolving emergency lights alternately shadowing and illuminating our hate-contorted faces in harsh bursts of red, and with our glee audible in our ritualistic chanting, this crowd could easily have been mistaken for any blood-crazed lynch mob in history. The only thing wrong with the scene was that the mob was an audience at an artistic performance and the streetsweeper was the mechanical kind, a huge yellow truck with a water tank and large metal brushes. The chant had started spontaneously, from our side of the fence, and caught on right away.

"GET the streetsweeper! KILL the streetsweeper!" As we chanted (yes, we of the Anthropology Club were aware we had crossed a crucial interior boundary in our dalliance with participant-observation), two robots moved in, through billows of red smoke, while one, two, three industrial-strength air-raid sirens cranked up the scale of apocalyptic noises. One robot dragged the unmanned vehicle forward while the other performed a menacing war-dance, responding to the crowd's hoarse goads by telescoping its battering ram and advancing on its prey. The killer 'bot slowly extended a solid metal bar, six or seven feet long and as thick as a human neck. At one end of the rod was a rotor assembly, but instead of blades or wings, a half dozen thick chains with lumps of metal at the ends hung limply like a monstrous cat-o'-nine-tails until the auto-flail motor kicked in.

The crowd was San Franciscan, and we weren't kidding: One of the municipal peculiarities of this locale is the city's penchant for firing the people who used to do a great job sweeping the street-debris into bright orange bags, replacing them with these lumbering vehicles that wet the street debris with sprinklers on the front and rotated it with wire brushes on the back, a process that turned entire neighborhoods into no-parking zones on street-cleaning day. When you have to move your car from in front of your own house at five in the morning, then lie in bed, listening to the sound of a half ton of Brillo on wet asphalt, one day out of seven, you can generate some genuine animosity when you see one of those vehicles at bay. Suddenly, the idea of violent public execution of hated machines seemed attractive, even natural.

This ritual did a frighteningly thorough job of stirring up everybody's latent feelings of technological blood-lust, tapping some kind of deep gut hostility to the stupidity of machines, coupled with a sick fascination with their destructive power. Someone ran into no-man's land, between the high-command bunker, the audience, and the killer robots. With the smoke and the screaming and the engines revving up, it was hard to tell whether it was a member of the SRL crew or an *espontaneo*. The mysterious stranger signalled the beginning of an all-out mechanical assault by hurling a sledgehammer at the windshield of the hated captive streetsweeper. The sound of the audience, responding as if from a single throat, was nauseating, joyous, hysterical, and especially frightening when we realized we, ourselves, were screaming at the top of our lungs but simply couldn't hear our own voices. The large robot cranked up the flails to attack speed, moving in like a gargantuan weed-eater until the whirling chains brought the first of the fist-sized hunks of metal into the windshield, throwing showers of fractured safety glass into the air.

When the noise died, the cold began to sink in. With the performing area reduced to a stinking heap of smoldering rubble and the crowd lifted to a height of primal overamped adrenal catharsis, then dropped into the reality of 3 A.M., there was nothing to do but turn around in silence and stumble toward our cars. There was nothing much to say until the ringing in our ears died down. As soon as I unpried my fingers from their grip on the chainlink fence and turned to leave, someone whose face I didn't see handed me a small matchbox-sized container. I shook it. Nothing rattled. I looked at it, noted that it was a clever kind of flyer of some kind, and put it in my pocket.

The next day, when I reached in my pocket, looking for something else, I pulled out an unexpected object. It was a matchbox, made of flimsy cardboard, covered by a photocopy of a scanning electron photomicrographic image of a gang of viruses. Printed notices covered four sides.

I held the box up to the light and took a close look at one of the two broader sides, which said: "HLIV—Human Lust Inducing Virus—developed by OK GENETIC ENGINEERING to solve an important world problem—what to do when he/she just wants to be friends. IMPORTANT—OK GENETIC ENGINEERING has no idea how this product will effect the ecological balance in Northern California. DO NOT OPEN THIS BOX without reading the warning on the back!"

I turned it over. The proclamation on the other side said: "WARNING—OK GENETIC ENGINEERING has not received permission to release this organism from NIH. We used a Stanford patent without paying the license fee, and we do not know how to file an Environmental Impact Statement. We are distributing HLIV free. Please make your own decision whether or not to release these organisms."

I read the message on one of the narrow sides, where the match-striker would be, and it said: "This box contains at least 220 HLIV virions in culture." On the other narrow side: "OK GENETIC ENGINEERING—J. P. Malloy, Pres.—'Quality Clones Since 1984.'" I opened it. Inside, a neatly typed label, glued to the bottom of the matchbox, said: "uh-oh." It was like getting a message from an apollonian evangelist on the way home from a dionysian rapture.

I keep the box on a shelf, near the couch where guests sit down in my living room, and use it as an observational instrument. Not one person has failed to open it.

PART 2

OVER THE EDGE OF
SCIENCE

The Smell of Things to Come

Forget extrasensory perception and turn your attention to smell, that wallflower of senses, for true telepathy resides in the nose. The discovery of *pheromones*—odors that transmit messages— heralds the most important breakthrough in communication since the first cave dweller learned to get what he wanted by grunting rhythmically. An ancient language still lingers in our nostrils, whether our forebrains know it or not.

It now appears that the nose, along with certain tufts of body hair, may be the antennae for a bionic communication network, a chemical switchboard linking you and me to every other walking, crawling, slithering, hopping, and flying thing on this planet. Molecular message packets wafting in the breeze are telling us all what to do, when to do it, and who to do it with. In terms of sex, birth, death, social organization—all of our most intimate and mortal activities—the implications of nasal communication are eerie, indeed.

I first learned about pheromones from a friend of mine who gets laid a lot. We had been playing squash all afternoon and were both preparing for a Saturday night of recreational heterosexuality. Before his perfunctory thirty-second shower, my friend Walter wiped his armpits with a white linen hand-kerchief. While I spent half an hour washing, deodorizing, shaving, after-shaving and mouthwashing, old Walt just folded his drenched handkerchief and carefully placed it in his shirt pocket.

"I found it in *Psychopathia Sexualis*," Walter claimed, when I inquired about the stinky-hanky routine. One of Walter's quirks is an inordinate affection for archaic erotica, so I was only mildly surprised when he began reciting Krafft-Ebing by heart: "A sensual young peasant revealed that he had excited many a chaste girl sexually, and easily gained his end, by carrying a handkerchief in his axilla for a time, while dancing, and then wiping his partner's perspiring face with it." Walter paused for a most convincing lecherous grin: "I tried it. It works."

"What's *axilla?*" I asked.

"Krafft-Ebing for armpit."

Walt's track record was unassailable, but I couldn't quite buy his scientific references, even when he threw in a corroborating passage from Casanova. That's when he hit me with phero-mones. "Why don't you ask Dr. Johnny about pheromones?" Walter jeered, sauntering off to another of his depressingly successful sexual excursions. Pheromones weren't in the dictionary, and since Walter's weekend once again made mine look co-matose, I decided to consult our friendly neighborhood scientist first thing Monday morning.

Dr. Johnny is a research type rather than a beeper-wearing-and-surgery doctor, so he can usually be found in his lab cu-bicle on the eleventh floor of our local medical complex. I found him in a crowded elevator, enroute to his lab. "Dr. Johnny," I pleaded shamelessly, right there, surrounded closely by all those whitecoats between floors: "You have to help me. I think I have pheromones. Or maybe I don't have enough of them. In any case . . . what *are* they?"

"Panic in a stalled elevator is a good candidate for pheromone-mediated behavior," he answered, much too loudly, just before we arrived at the eleventh floor. "Of course, we might, heh heh, have to fake a few accidents, then take blood samples to find out." I'm sure the other passengers were relieved to see us leave that elevator.

"It isn't my specialty, you understand, but it isn't very hard to learn most of the evidence for human pheromones, since there is so little of it. At the moment, human pheromones are in the theoretical stage, just as nuclear reactors and lunar landers used to be. It's the very beginning of a brand-new science, and the findings are fragmentary but intriguing. In 1971, it was observed that coeds in dormitories synchronized their menstrual cycles. Hmmmm. Just how did all those bodies communicate with one another? And there is a demonstrated correlation between mammalian sex hormone cycles and sensitivity to odors. Hmmm and ahh. In the late 1970s, an aerosol aphrodisiac was first marketed—for pig breeding. Pheromones have a very rich research and development future, believe me. If it doesn't revolutionize the perfume industry, you can be sure that commercial exploitation of pheromones will have an impact on animal husbandry."

Johnny's answer was characteristically tangential, but my next educated guess was on target: "Pheromones are hormones you can smell?"

"Close. You could taste them, as well. And they are like hormones because they are chemical messages that affect the behavior of the organism that senses them. For that matter, you don't even have to consciously sense them to be affected. The interesting thing to a biochemist of my persuasion is the *way* they work. All these very complex behavior chains seem to be triggered by nothing more than a pattern in space. In plants and insects, it appears that the effect of pheromones depends on the *shape* of the molecule. The fragrance of a rose, for example, is an effect of a ten-carbon chain that is arranged in a specific geometric configuration. If you could arrange your own carbon molecules into the same spatial configuration, it would end up smelling like a rose."

"But why would a flower want to send aerosol telegrams?" I asked.

"I suspect that the message is intended for our old friends, the birds and the bees." Johnny dropped his voice level when he lumbered into his laboratory. "The message is something simple, like: 'Rose here. Come and get some pollen on your proboscis.'"

When Dr. Johnny started reaching for his reagents, I knew the audience was ending. As I made my exit, only slightly less puzzled than before, he gave me one last piece of advice: "Pheromonically speaking, insects are where the action is." Then he disappeared into his universe of carbon chains and molecular geometry.

I took his advice and questioned the first entomologist I could find who knew how to spell *pheromone*. We talked for hours, and that night I did not sleep well; my dreams were a montage of every 1950s insect mutant movie I'd ever seen. Grasshoppers, ants, and bees, all spraying invisible smelly messages to one another, had taken over the world—well, at least my subconscious.

Insect experts are notoriously touchy about human analogies, particularly where pheromones are concerned. Still, the possibilities are fascinating. Take ants, for example. Lewis Thomas, in *Lives of a Cell*, first brought the pheromonal implications of their behavior to public attention. Ants as isolated individuals are too stupid to stay alive for long; they have been likened to ganglia on legs. As a group, though, ants are far too human for comfort. They practice agriculture, raise livestock, wage war, employ slaves, bridge rivers, and appear to produce just about everything people produce, except television game shows, intercontinental ballistic missiles, and pinball machines.

Watch a line of ants in action and you'll notice that they rub antennae a lot. When two or three randomly groping ants stumble into proximity, an exchange of pheromones directs them into a slightly more ordered unit. As more and more workers drift into the project, a kind of community odor accumulates, triggering progressively more complex behavior chains. Mindless food-seeking becomes a supply line. A bunch of insects pushing around grains of sand slowly becomes a team of architects.

The mind that directs this process is not easy to conceive, for the ant brain does not reside in the nerve tissue of the individual ants but in a network of pheromones. The mind of an anthill is a silent, invisible, chemical telegraph; one ant can transmit only one letter, but three ants can send a syllable, and a million can formulate military strategy.

Pheromone-regulated behavior is not confined to insects. Spawning salmon are able to recognize the taste of the old home stream in dilutions weaker than one part per billion. The next time you eat lox and bagels, don't forget that your breakfast has a homing mechanism more sensitive than that of a cruise missile, and all because of its smell sensors. Once they cross a chemical boundary, wolf packs will abandon wounded game, even in the midst of a famine. Rats in a cage will eat one another when they breed past a certain limit. Dogs urinate on your leg because you are a territorial boundary; fire hydrants are canine olfactory U.N. meetings.

Biochemical messages are often incredibly potent: A single molecule of *bombykol*, a synthetic sex-attractant for moths, can draw an amorous male moth from miles away. Each female moth carries a trillion-dose payload of this thermonuclear come-hither juice. Someday, a graduate student is going to drop a flask of that stuff and become the first human to smother under a ton of horny moths.

Pheromones seem to act as a communal adhesive, holding together and shaping the group behavior of packs, swarms, and flocks of insects and animals; they might well function similarly in families, tribes, and nations of humans. If chemical regulation turns out to be as pervasive in our own species as it is in other species, then we humans may have to recast our fundamental beliefs about sex, society, and the future of civilization.

When we start to study sex-attractants, the urge to anthropomorphize becomes especially urgent. Sex, free will, and body odor are delicate subjects in our culture. When you bring them together, a weird kind of critical mass is achieved. The big guns of modern sex science have received research grants for years from International Flavors and Fragrances, Inc., the giant of the tongue and nose business. A variety of commercial institutions have funded research into human pheromones. It isn't hard to guess what these researchers' commercial backers are after—the discovery of a true airborne aphrodisiac (or *an*aphrodisiac, the ultimate contraceptive) could set off a social explosion that would make the last sexual revolution look like a Victorian tea party.

The aphrodisiac qualities of human odors were noted as early as the Old Testament: the Song of Solomon, that oft-cited bit of Biblical erotica, makes reference to a sexual "myrrh." Henry III of France is said to have conceived a royal passion after a hanky-sniffing incident. In *Against the Grain*, the underground masterpiece of olfacto-literary decadence, author J. K. Huysmans created an elaborate, oddly prophetic smell-fantasy. You can be sure that the perfumers are paying renewed attention to such fables.

The question still remains, however: Do human pheromones really exist, or are we merely engaged in wish-fulfilling fantasies? Humans are rather more complicated than insects, especially when it comes to sexual behavior, but that commercial spray-can essence of pig sex, originally isolated from the breath of lusty male hogs, is also found in human urine. Over the past ten years, hundreds of similar substances have been found in human perspiration and genital secretions—function unknown.

The first text on pheromones, published in 1974, featured

long sections on insect, plant, and animal studies, and a single chapter on "The Likelihood of Human Pheromones." The author, curiously enough, was Alex Comfort, the author of the best-selling *Joy of Sex*. Comfort presented a compelling case for the existence of human pheromones, basing his argument on the continuing evolutionary survival of body hair and apocrine glands located near erogenous zones. "A conspicuous and apparently unused antenna array presupposes an unsuspected communications system" is the way Dr. Comfort put it.

In 1979, a team at Warwick University in England, led by George Dodd, identified two compounds in human sweat closely related to the commercial pig-attractant. They managed to synthesize one of the compounds, *alpha androstenol*, a chemical related to the androgens, the male sex hormones. The effects of this suspected human sex pheromone was tested in a number of ways. When it was clandestinely sprayed in the air, both men and women rated photographs of women to be sexier and more attractive than the same photographs which were judged in unsprayed rooms. When it was sprayed on theater seats, chair in waiting rooms, and telephone booths, there was a marked increase in the time of occupancy of both sexes, but women appeared to be more strongly drawn to those places.

In 1986, researchers at the Monell Chemical Senses Center and the University of Pennsylvania School of Medicine might have lit the fuse for the least expected social upheaval of the 1990s with their evidence that, according to a report in *Time* magazine, December 1, 1986, "women who have sex with men at least once a week are more likely to have normal menstrual cycles, fewer infertility problems and a milder menopause than celibate women and women who have sex rarely or sporadically." Of course, if this is true and if it is pheromone-linked, then women won't necessarily require a male partner to keep her endocrine system well-tuned. In the same *Time* report, Winnifred Cutler, a biologist and specialist in behavioral endocrinology who conducted the study along with organic chemist

George Preti, stated: "If you look at all the data, the conclusion is compelling. A man or his essence seems essential for an optimally fertile system. . . . My dream is that manufactured male essence, in creams, sprays or perfumes, can dramatically alter the well-being of women."

The Monell Center has filed applications for four pheromone patents. A Japanese concern has purchased rights for research and marketing of products based on their discoveries. Despite the success of the researchers at the Monell Center, the effects and interactions of over two-hundred components of male and female odors remain largely unknown. It won't be easy, but it looks possible: When the professionals finally track down Casanova's secret ingredient, we may have the opportunity to saturate ourselves with true essence of sex, and it will undoubtedly be marketed at the highest price the market will bear.

Although the science of pheromones is still in its infancy, a billion-dollar industry is devoted to the promotion of products intended to mask or destroy human odors. The most alarming side effect of deodorant pollution is related to the hypothesis that human sex-linked odors are produced with the cooperation of symbiotic bacteria—those nasty little "underarm" germs we are still being trained to kill.

Our conveniently moist skin folds and strategically located patches of hair are at least circumstantial evidence that these bacteria are true symbiotic partners that may, in fact, be necessary for the satisfactory consummation of the human mating ritual. When our underarm symbiotes are eliminated, will we still remember how to reproduce?

The possibility of extraconscious chemical communication beyond the sexual realm is a tempting hypothesis. Pheromones could account for the volatile and mysterious chemistry between people that is so often misinterpreted by spoken language. What are olfactory messages, after all, but a form of extrasensory or supersensory perception? There may be an entirely new science waiting to be born—the parapsychology of the nose. There is something arcane and fascinating about the possibility of re-educating the human nose, regaining the lost language that lurks about in buried layers of our brains. What invisible intercourse did we abandon when humans began to speak?

Or did we begin to lose touch with our noses when we began to wear clothing? Part of the evolutionary purpose of the male sexual organ is to deposit urine-carried messages. Surely, every man must wonder at one time or another about that final spasm that usually lands a couple of telltale drops on his foot or pants leg. Apparently, we use our own clothing in much the same way dogs use fire hydrants.

If human pheromonal perception exists, it is highly likely that olfactory sensitivity can be trained. The sense of smell is more responsive to education than any of our other senses, because a portion of the sensing organ itself permanently changes to fit the specifications of each new odor, a system which makes it possible for mammals to discriminate between hundreds of thousands of odors.

When specific human pheromones are identified, the technique of gas chromatography will become a powerful tool—or possible weapon—in the armory of behavioral science. "Odor fingerprinting" technology has been steadily advancing in accuracy; chemical traces in the atmosphere can now be analyzed at dilutions measured in parts per billion. Certain pheromone combinations might serve as "smell fingerprints," indicators of unique personal biochemical patterns that might reveal a great deal about the person under olfactory scrutiny.

The odors a person emits are the product of that person's metabolism—their body chemistry. If it is possible to speculate about people's metabolism by analyzing their odors, it is also possible to make some predictions about their moods. Mood analysis and mood adjustment of individuals, groups, perhaps entire cities, could be accomplished at a distance with the proper pheromones. What if the air inside a boxing ring during a heavyweight fight could be analyzed, synthesized, and issued to infantry before combat? Whole new group highs might become the rage, from *Essence of Honeymoon* to *Eau de Board Meeting*.

The opposite line of extrapolation leads to the paranoid utopia where a dreamlike odor makes it feel oh-so-nice to be a drone. It might become possible to literally lead us by our noses. Nasal fascism might not be too far away, technologically speaking: If *trans-3-methyl-hexenoic acid* sounds like the latest terror drug, your nose is already steering you in the right direction, for it is one of the chemicals that lend a distinctive odor to the sweat of schizophrenics. A little of that stuff in the air-conditioning ought to make anybody nervous.

There is a hopeful as well as a sinister side to metabolic fingerprinting. Physical and even mental health might be restored by rebalancing chemical messages. Drugs might be customized, tailored to the special body chemistry of each patient. Allergies, donor compatibility for organ transplants, perhaps even sexual compatibility, could be determined at a distance. The possible role of pheromones in symbiosis, the enigmatic process by which separate organs share and exchange life functions, might shed light on one of the most vital questions of cancer research: How does the immune system discriminate between host organism and invader, between self and not-self? Could unconscious pheromonal manipulation explain faith-healing and the "laying on of hands" that doctors and witch doctors alike rely on for diagnosis? (Indeed, Tibetan medicine uses the odor of the patient's urine as a diagnostic instrument.)

Consider the smell of death. New studies of the death process, prompted by the testimony of thousands who have clinically "died," then were restored to life by modern medical techniques, suggest that physical crises can trigger a kind of "death hormone" that soothes pain, slows time, and expands awareness. Is there a corresponding pheromone, a biochemical last will and testament? If there are a few molecules from Leonardo and Adolf and Jesus in each breath we take, are there any instructions tagging along?

From the beginning of our lives until the end, we are bombarded by chemical messages from other people, animals, even plants. The most generalized chemical communication imaginable, the grand switchboard connecting all life into a global society, is the basis of another infant science named *allelochemics*. Electromagnetic signals, as well as chemical messages, are exchanged among the interacting components of any ecosystem. Even simple grasses emit signals that announce availability to potential symbiotes and set limits on the encroachment of predators. Evolving populations regulate each other through the messages they exchange, balancing "Let's mate" with "Let's fight." Sometimes the message is "Eat me; I'm overpopulated."

The dance of predator and prey is orchestrated by a billion chemical fiddlers. In a unit as large as a forest, a jungle, or a planet, entire symphonies of information resonate through the air, an inaudible behavioral ballet, choreographed by countless biochemical transactions. If the other life forms plugged into the allelomone hotline have a way of talking back to humans, it is likely that the message is already planted in each one of us, waiting to be triggered. If the ultimate human pheromone is population-fused, as it seems to be with rats and lemmings, apocalypse is just a nose away.

What do you call a global pheromone? Or a cosmic pheromone? If such philosophically disturbing beasties exist, we humans are involved from our armpits to the ozone layer. Radiotelescopes already sweep the skies in search of alien messages; perhaps it is time to search for *terrestrial* messages. In the strange days to come, it might not be a bad idea to build a pheromonal doomsday detector.

The most sophisticated odor-sensing system known to man is the nose and olfactory lobe of the common bunny rabbit. If rapid growth of receptor cells (the part of the nose which responds to a new smell) is what determines an organism's "smell intelligence," then rabbits could qualify as olfactory geniuses, with an estimated 100 million olfactory cells. Perhaps the day will come when a rabbit's nose is interfaced to a computer. When such an organic pheromone forecaster comes into existence, somebody should ask it how many humans this planet can take before the big stink appears and we go the way of the lemmings or the dinosaurs.

The day the human hivemind happens, don't be surprised if you don't hear a bang. There won't even be a whimper. It will all start with a funny smell.

What Causes Anger?

The three horsemen of the twentieth century—anger, anxiety, and stress—ride through the modern no-man's-land where our carnivorous past battles our philosophic present. We're all riding biological battlewagons, and we don't know how to turn them off in polite company, so we collectively consume several *billion* tranquillizers each year. Anger is as deeply rooted as the survival instinct: Blame it on the era of the dinosaurs, on air conditioning and glandular secretions, on social repression and positive ions. It's no wonder we're all so steamed up, with a hundred million years stepping on our backs.

Back in the hairy old primeval, while we trekked away the millennia on the savannah trying to think of what to do with the real estate, there were only three possible ways to greet a strange man or beast: You either ripped the fellow's throat out, got the hell out of his neighborhood, or banded together with him to hunt some bison and maybe grow a little corn. Now that the bison are gone and the corn comes in cans, the action has moved from the savannah to the seventeenth floor, and social relations aren't as simple as they used to be.

Every time a stranger intrudes on your space, you just can't rip his or her throat out or hightail it down the road. When those prehistoric carnivorous hormones gush through your bloodstream, your newer brain centers strive to override instinct with cognition. When culture prevails over adrenaline, you get angry instead of bloody, you avoid social disruption, and you have a running start on arterial disease.

We're dealing here with an evolutionary generation gap within our own anatomy. The fight-or-flight response is a marvelous survival reflex, originally elaborated in the age of the reptiles; anger, however, is a relatively new category, a product of the brash young neocortex. Anger is what happens when a defense system evolves far enough to think about itself. It's the psychic price we pay for that elevator ride from hunting and gathering to wheeling and dealing.

Hand-to-hand combat has been the human way of resolving conflict for a very long time. But our weapons and our way of life evolved too fast for our physiological habits. In our present era, the ultimate aggression is global suicide. On the individual level, humanity now frowns upon unauthorized mayhem, which puts us all into conflict with ourselves every day. When that old reptilian fight-or-flight collides with those newfangled social rules, you get your anger, your ulcers, your paranoia, and your arteriosclerosis. Anger is the visible fraction of a many-tentacled bioweapon, an internal supercharger that keeps you alive long enough to reproduce—and then eats your heart out.

Human brains didn't simply materialize from the primordial soup one day. It took a few billion years to get from amino acids to thermonuclear warheads. Defense systems were in on the brain-building game from the start; even the genetic code has its military-industrial complex. The combination of spinal cord, hindbrain and midbrain—which still partially controls the human panic button—came into its own around the time of the great reptiles. The reptilian brain is still with us today, embedded in our skulls, although it is now shackled and bound by its younger relatives, the limbic system and neocortex.

"Eat this; flee that; mate now" pretty well sums up the dinosaurian way of thinking, a philosophy that prevailed longer than any of us would care to admit. It was a nice little basic brain, far beyond the capabilities of today's best robot builders; it kept the heart beating, the lungs breathing, the mouth chewing, and the species reproducing. (An unwritten corollary of Darwin's theory of natural selection is that any individual too dumb or unmotivated to mate automatically forfeits its place in the gene pool.)

Things tend to change when those notoriously mutable chromosomes have a few hundred million years to combine and recombine, dream and scheme. On the planet of the dinosaurs, vicious little evolutionary variations like mammals began to dominate the scene. That's when emotions joined the big ball of defense systems, and rage became the newest neural wrinkle.

One hundred and fifty million years ago, give or take an eon, some maverick reptile brains grew a surrounding layer of tissue—the limbic system. With the limbic system you get your endocrine glands, amygdala, and hormones. The limbic level is where all kinds of neurochemical hell and bizarre behavior erupt. In a previous episode of the current era—the early 1960s—the age of the random mass murderer was kicked off by an Eagle Scout. It was a tumor in the amygdala that sent Charles Whitman up to the University of Texas bell tower with a batbag full of ammo and a couple of carbines. You'll never catch a reptile doing anything like that.

With the cetaceans (whales and dolphins) and the higher primates (apes and astronauts), the neocortex (Latin for "new rind") took the helm of the reptilian/mammalian brain. Barely a million years ago, when *Homo sap* began to differentiate itself as a species, the self-defense and brain-building processes came into exquisite collision. Reptiles were capable of dimwitted murder; mammals were able to feel hot and bothered about it; but only humans were able to *think* about it, reflect on it, plan to do it again.

Consciousness, that epiphenomenon of too much brain

tissue, made for a new, highly efficient killer species. But premeditation also made it possible for individuals to override both instinct and emotion by means of abstract metaprograms like the Ten Commandments. Moral choice became possible, and the first ulcer was born.

Stress is amplified when an organism thinks it has free will; it's a matter of all the conflicting decisions it has to make. For simpler organisms, the fight-or-flight reflex is cued to specific perceptual triggers. For a frog sitting placidly by the pond, all the roaring in the world isn't going to make a dent in its concentration, but the optical configuration of a snake (or a garden hose) will initiate frantic hopping toward the nearest deep water. Rabbits panic at the sight of rapidly moving shadows. The nature of perceptual warning arrays becomes less specific and more generalized as one moves up the evolutionary ladder. For people, the perceptual configuration that triggers fight or flight could be *anything*, depending on your interpretation.

To one person, the sight of a man on horseback is comforting, but to another, it means impending doom. That's what happens when your self-defending biorobot evolves enough brain tissue to generalize its reaction. Individuals no longer inherit their reactions, they *learn* them. Interpretation is the supreme neocortical function and is often a pain in the amygdala. When your interpretations are too creative, you edge into paranoia. When your interpretations aren't creative enough, you die young and that means you don't get a chance to pass any more stupid chromosomes down the line.

The constant bickering between the older and newer divisions of the human brain sets off dozens of hormonal false alarms in the course of a normal day. While your heart is beating and your conscious mind is thinking, the rest of you is scanning the horizon for danger. Interpretation could override reaction but never could replace it. Inside the meekest man is a half-billion years of anatomy looking for trouble, and every one of his perceptual centers has a direct line to the alarm system (what was that sound? look at that! it smells like smoke!).

Self-defense responses are great for individual survival in a dangerous environment, but unrequited anger in a socially constrained environment is a known killer. The requirements of species survival don't include personal longevity. This phenomenon is most evident in certain species of fish, which die within hours of spawning, aging with superaccelerated rapidity after the long, hard, swim upstream and the all-too-brief consummation. Evolution doesn't care about any organism's lifespan after it passes the age of fertility. As soon as we add our crucial increments to the nucleic message pool, we could disintegrate like so many salmon and the human species would do just fine. Our defense systems evolved to keep us alive long enough to spawn. After that, it's every organ for itself.

Now that we have chosen to repress our instincts in favor of civilized behavior, the systems that constantly fought attacks from the outside have turned into a threat themselves; they are attacking from within. There is no malevolent intent—anger eats you because it has to eat *something*. The strange thing about our neocortical age is the evidence that the way you think about anger may determine how long you will live and how you will die. It has to do with how you deal with your addiction to your own internal thrill-drugs.

ANATOMY OF AN ADRENALINE FLASH

We might not face the sabertooth every day, but freeways and urban turf offer ample opportunity for hot-flashing. Modern chemical euphoriants like cocaine can't compare with the raw brain-burning ecstasy of adrenaline—the hundred-million-year-old high. It may be considered a cheap kick today, but adrenaline was the original mother of invention. Even today, our lives depend on thousands of short hormone jags, plus a couple of hotshots of the pure stuff at critical moments.

Consider your well-known "ninety-pound housewife lifts car off son's chest" story from the inside out. First, the senses relay a potent image to all parts of her brain: "My kid is being crunched." The intellectual centers in her cortex understand that this is a bad situation, soon to get worse. The emotional centers in her limbic system sense that this is cause for a brief period of emotional numbness, followed by a radical emotional reaction. The reptilian brain, not burdened by introspection time, has already voted for metabolic combat status.

When her higher and lower brain centers agree that this is an emergency, they trigger the red button in the hypothalamus and call in the heavies from the endocrine system. Electrochemical signals race through neural pathways, and the infantry of the hormonal world—adrenaline and noradrenaline—pour into the bloodstream and surge to the big biochemical staging ground in the liver.

Within the liver is an emergency fuel depot in the form of stored glycogen molecules. When the adrenaline, released at the receipt of a panic signal from higher centers, hits the liver, the stored glycogen is reconverted to "burnable" glucose and distributed through the bloodstream. The first tidal wave of muscular energy as the ninety-pound housewife grabs the automobile's bumper comes from the immediate glucose discharge. The euphoria that often follows the accomplishment of prodigious physical feats is a side effect of that first adrenaline-glucose implosion. Your hypothetical supermom needs a hefty portion of her liver's output when she hefts that auto. She'll also need an extraordinary performance by her heart and lungs to provide extra oxygen for the sudden metabolic storm.

In case of a serious situation, you get your noradrenaline, which helps activate free fatty acids to fuel muscle work. Elevated levels of free fatty acid also make blood platelets clump together more readily than usual. It's very handy to have good, thick, quick-clotting blood if your arm is about to be ripped off in mortal combat; but if it happens too often without immediate heavy muscle work to burn the fuel, the free fatty acids help deposit cholesterol in unhealthy places like the arteries. The bill for forty years of suppressed hormone flashes comes due at the cardiologist.

If you ate the pulsing heart of your opponent every time you got angry, your conscience might bother you, but your body would get along just fine. Every time you're aroused to anger and do not translate that emotion into immediate, violent physical activity, your body gets another dose of slow poison. While you are steaming at your desk, fuming behind the wheel of your car, or enraged in the comfort of your own home, your gastric juices eat at your stomach lining, your free fatty acids besludge your arteries, while your liver, lungs, and heart work overtime detoxifying your blood.

Repression is unavoidable. If the source is your spouse, your boss, your child, or a burly stranger, then there are very good reasons for not acting out feelings of rage. It does no good to deny anger, but it pays to be aware of the psychic and metabolic debt you build up with each swallowed word, every clenched fist. Sooner or later, in one way or another, that mortal debt has to be paid.

Because interpretation is the trigger for our primeval reaction mechanisms, one's personal attitudes toward stress-inducing stimuli—one's philosophy of life—can determine whether the by-products of our instincts eat us, cleanse us, or turn us on. When it was discovered by medical researchers that the tense, driven, highly competitive, highly internalized lifestyle so prized in our society characterizes the potentially fatal condition now known as Type A behavior, the benefits of meditative, relaxing activities—what Harvard researchers call The Relaxation Response—were extolled in best sellers and Sunday supplements.

The links between stress and disease are well documented. But other intriguing, unsuspected links might exist between anger and orgasm, to pick one explosive example. Adrenaline isn't the only hormone we secrete on a sunny spring day. Don't forget the gonads and their proud product testosterone, the hormone of male honor.

Recent observations and experiments with higher primates suggest that testosterone, the male sex hormone, aside from its primary sexual effects also acts as both incentive and reward for aggression. Primate males tend to fight more when their hormone levels are high, and the victors of battles tend to have higher hormone levels than the losers. Thirty seconds of observing a modern male in the throes of *Monday Night Football* is convincing (if indirect) evidence that the primate findings extrapolate to the human condition. The sad truth seems to be that humans fight so much because so many males find fighting sexy. If anybody ever decides to invent a "moral alternative to war," like that called for by William James, they better take masculine hormonal peculiarities into account.

Orgasm, panic, heroism, rage, and other strong feelings share some interesting common neural pathways. The connection between sex and aggression will be pursued down different theoretical paths in the near future, when biochemistry gives social scientists powerful tools they never had before. The actual relationships between hormones and behavior are only beginning to be discovered. Many of the stickiest social issues of the day—male-dominance hierarchies, human territoriality, the origins of aggression—may be tied up in an intricate metabolic chain somewhere between lust and anger.

On the other hand, maybe our hormones aren't entirely to blame. It's a pretty aggravating world out there—down to the air we breathe.

*　　*　　*

ANGER IS BLOWING IN THE WIND

There was a desert wind blowing that night. It was one of those hot dry Santa Anas that come down through the mountain passes and curl your hair and make your nerves jump and your skin itch. On nights like that every booze party ends in a fight. Meek little wives feel the edge of the carving knife and study their husbands' necks. Anything can happen.

—Philip Marlowe in Raymond Chandler's *Red Wind*

Raymond Chandler was hip to the ugly side-effects of the Santa Ana winds, and so were the native California tribes, a thousand years before Marlowe cast his jaundiced gaze on hazy L.A. Shamans, surgeons, hunters, and farmers have always known about the savage bewitchment of man and beast that precedes a monsoon and the mental and physical plagues that ride on certain hot mountain winds. To this day, those Middle Eastern countries in the path of the khamsin exercise judicial leniency for minor crimes of violence committed when the evil winds blow.

Today, you don't even have to live in the path of the mistral in France, the sirocco in Italy, the foehn in Switzerland and Austria or the Santa Ana in Southern California to experience the kind of weather that puts people a twitch away from berserk. We have something called "urban microclimate" today, and it does to the fellows on the seventeenth floor what the khamsin does to the fellahin down by the Nile.

The physical phenomena that link the weather to our moods have to do with a very faint but vital component of the air we breathe—charged ions. In each cubic centimeter of atmosphere, there are normally only one or two thousand positively and negatively charged ions—much lonelier than a peanut in a ball park, from the molecular point of view. Experimentation has shown that plants wither and animals can die when they breathe air that is normal in every other respect, except that most of the negatively charged particles have been removed. When the usual five-to-four positive-negative ion ratio is altered, suicide or lyric poetry ensues, depending on the nature of the alteration.

The evil winds contain a large number of positively charged particles, and subsequent research has confirmed that large positive-ion concentrations can induce everything from depression and migraine to impotence and rage, especially in the people who are allergic or sensitive to this change—which amounts to approximately one-quarter of the general population.

Conversely, a slightly elevated ratio of negative ions seems to make some people feel absolutely cheerful, just a touch short of euphoric. Hot winds that carry a lot of sand or rub against mountains tend to generate a large positive-ion concentration. Gentler, cooler breezes near running water, like the air near a waterfall or the seashore, tend to produce a much more amicable ratio of negative ions. A ski slope, a meadow on a spring day—places people traditionally go to relax, unwind, and feel good—are rich sources of such airborne well-being.

The first collections of symptoms and personal accounts of people who are allergic to evil winds sound like catalogs of the range of stress-related diseases. The etiology of many stress-related illnesses closely resembles the effects of positive-ion allergy. Could it be that a subliminal tinkering with the endocrine system produces both the beneficial and deleterious effects of atmospheric ions?

This is all new territory, medically speaking. But if the ion-endocrine connection is indeed a good guess at the mechanism, it is possible that positive ions (the ones that drive you amok) have a cumulative microtriggering effect on stress responses. A continuous flow of subconscious danger alarms could permanently elevate hormone levels, thus keeping the hapless air-breathing organism in a permanent state of near-rage or near-fear.

That means you and me—and it's happening right here in urban America. Megalopoli produce an unplanned but psychologically potent microclimate of their own. Life in big cities, in sealed skyscrapers and air-conditioned factories, has changed the content of the air we breathe. Our own species and all other aerobic life on earth evolved in an atmosphere that has contained a certain ion content. The physical presence of cities, combined with industrial pollution and local weather conditions, can produce long periods of positive-ion overdose, affecting tens of millions of people at a time. Ask a New York cop what it's like after midnight in August, when the temperature has been in the nineties for a few days.

It doesn't stop with the air you breathe outside or in the office. The psychological ill effects of fluorescent lighting overdose, for example, are only beginning to be understood. Besides bad ions, artificial lighting, reptile brains, and toxic hormones, you can identify a dozen free-floating anger stimuli right in your own home. If you find yourself overwhelmed by enigmatic hostility, it could be noise pollution, the full moon, biorhythmic irregularity, high pollen counts, microwave radiation, sunspot cycles, fluoridation, cosmic-ray showers, or even your family dog at the root of it all.

Whatever the causes of anger, there are sound medical reasons for finding a way to neutralize the toxic side effects. Think of anger as an intelligence test: If you fail to deal with it, you flunk. If you flunk, you multiply the odds that you will die young.

If you choose to deal with anger, there are any number of ways to neutralize those metabolic poisons: martial arts, massage, hang-gliding, meditation, whitewater rafting, Sunday painting, rock climbing, kazoo-playing, Marx Brothers movies—even a dry martini—can give you a healthy way to work off your endocrine overcharge. You're bucking a half-billion years of evolution and 90 percent of your instincts, but one good way to live to a ripe old age is to learn how to get properly pissed off.

Brave New Male

If you are one of the billion-odd adult earthlings who possess a penis, be prepared for some strange changes—soon. Thanks to a few quiet developments on several different scientific fronts, the future of masculinity is very much in question. Twentieth-century technology, from the birth-control pill to the waterbed, has kept us all too busy pondering what has *already* happened to our sex lives to worry about what *might* happen in the near future. Too bad, fellas. This little oversight could cost us our family jewels.

If we don't decide what to do with the new male biology before it figures out what to do with us, the man of tomorrow will be standing precisely where the data hits the fan. It is time for every man to take a close look at the implications behind the scientific papers, because many of the new biological spinoffs are aimed directly at our gonads.

Two equally mind-boggling alternatives are emerging from the murky borderland of sexual futurism: Delectable new dimensions of sensation might soon become part of every man's erotic repertoire—or the male body could mutate beyond recognition. What you and I know—or don't know—about our own sexual mechanism will determine which way our balls ultimately bounce.

In the more optimistic of these two parallel scenarios, men of the year 2000 could enjoy exotic extras like orgasmic earlobes, replaceable sex organs, electronic aphrodisiacs, ultrasensory intercourse, and a range of ecstasy options that would make current notions of kinkiness look sedate by comparison. Even now, there is talk in human-sexuality circles of creating the new "sensate male." Sexologists have observed, for example, that a number of paraplegics are able to experience sexual pleasure and even orgasm through stimulation of the neck, shoulders, chest, or whatever patch of skin is still sensitive. How would you like your *entire body* to become as sensitive as your penis? If you really want to work at it, such a state of sensitivity is possible, at least in theory.

"Theoretically, the entire body is an erogenous zone," notes Michael Rossman, a Berkeley sex therapist. "The brain, after all, is our most important sex organ. Yoga and biofeedback techniques suggest that new learning tools can be created in order to shape new sexual zones. By learning to reinterpret nerve sensations and by slowly coupling the idea of arousal to nongenital areas, it is entirely possible that the male of the future will be able to have as strong an orgasm from stimulating his earlobe as men currently experience from direct stimulation of the penis."

On the nastier side of the speculation is the distinct possibility that the man of the year 2000 might not exist at all, except in sperm banks, stored in insulated metal vessels at −197 degrees. Radical biologists (that is, people with knowledge of biological research, who also happen to have radical views on sexual politics) now see the male of our species as technically expendable, and a few of them are looking into the possibility of putting this theory into practice. While bioengineers put the finishing touches on the means to replace human males, their co-conspirators in the social sciences are coming up with reasons why the planet might be better off without masculinity as we now know it. Dr. John Money, one of the men responsible for the first sex-change surgery performed in the United States, has declared that masculinity as it is presently defined is more of a social fiction than a biological reality: "There are not two sexes," he stated in an interview in *Omni* magazine: "There is a continuum. You can't do a head count. It doesn't work that way. You don't even come up with fifteen or fifty different sexes. It looks like a spectrum."

At this moment, the forces of social transformation and the stainless steel artillery of laboratory science are both zeroing in on the question of what exactly makes a man a man. A secret war is brewing over some very near and dear territory—the shape of manhood to come. While the data are being gathered, the conclusions debated, and applications developed, we had all better prepare for the brave new male. If informed public opinion is to have any effect on the outcome of this battle, it is now up to lay males to understand our own sexual biology—before we wake up obsolete some morning.

Like any other seminormal twentieth centurian, I never thought that anyone was out to alter my most cherished equipment. The idea of messing around with masculinity surfaced toward the end of my bachelorhood, when I was attempting to seduce the biochemist who lived at the end of the hall in my building. It began as a pure, classical battle of the sexes: I plied her with martinis, and she told me about the plot to do away with men.

The deliciously mesmerizing Virginia L., Ph.D., was an expert on glandular secretions. She did things to rat pituitaries and hauled around thick fanfolds of computer printouts, but she didn't wear her white lab coat on the street—which gave her double credibility in my book. The only glandular secretions that concerned me that night were Virginia's, but she insisted on talking about redesigning my physiology.

"It isn't like there's a worldwide formal conspiracy of terrorist biochemists out to eliminate men—although more than a few of my colleagues would gladly join such a group," Virginia confided, after exactly one too many drinks. Then she told me about Doctor Money's statement and added that prominent feminist Andrea Dworkin wrote, in *Woman-Hating: A Radical Look at Sexuality*, that Money's research "threatens to transform the traditional biology of sex difference into the radical biology of sex similarity. That is not to say that there is one sex, but that there are many."

I tried to ignore the bizarre tack the conversation had taken. She was determined to drink me under the coffee table and enlighten me about the antisocial effects of my own hormones. I was determined to engage her in a serious experiment in telekinesis—moving her body out of the living room and through the bedroom door.

When she said something about "mandatory chemical castration," deep-seated instinctive fear blunted my strategy and awakened my curiosity. I made the fatal mistake of listening attentively.

"If an extreme man-hater with a biochemistry degree happened to take over the world, she would have the technical means for continuing the human species without any living males," Virginia asserted, perhaps a bit too enthusiastically. "Spermatazoa from eugenically ideal specimens could be stored in liquid nitrogen. At the rate of several hundred million sperm per ejaculation, it wouldn't take long to, uh—*collect*—an adequate seed stock. Yes, an Amazocracy could propagate quite easily with frozen husbands, until they crack the final problem of parthenogenesis."

I was forced to call a point of information. I didn't feel like losing face by admitting ignorance in such a personal area, but *parthenogenesis* sounded too ominous to let it pass.

"It is more commonly known as virgin birth," Virginia explained, "and only one woman in history has been believed to have accomplished it. Biologically speaking, parthenogenesis simply means life without father. When women learn how to make babies without heterosexual assistance, even at the cellular level, we won't need to keep all that expensive, perishable, frozen sperm around."

"Can't you scientists use your grants on more pleasant alternatives?" I'm ashamed to recall the involuntary tremor in my voice.

"If a sperm-bank future leaves you cold, how would you feel about self-regeneration of your penis?" she asked, as demurely as a lady can ask a question like that while a gentleman is trying to decide between quaking with fear and groping her leg.

"Depends on how it feels about me, I guess," was my weak try at a fast, unflustered comeback. It came out sounding a notch or three less cocky than I intended.

She deflected my humor with a smile so quick I almost missed it. "Regeneration experiments have been highly successful in rats and salamanders. Preliminary evidence indicates that electrical stimulation and chemotherapy can encourage regeneration of limbs in other species," she continued. "In London, two newborn infants, who had lost their fingers, regenerated them."

Replaceable penises? The implications are perversely enticing. It could eliminate the most primal of Freudian fears, certainly. Male behavior would be a whole different ball game without the castration complex. Better than psychological relief would be the prospect of interchangeable, home-grown organs in any size, shape, texture, color, or vibratory frequency we desire: one for everyday wear, and a selection of Saturday night specials. Expendable members, I was soon to learn, are not the only sensual possibilities lurking in the corridors of science.

By the time Virginia spread the word about me to some of her funny friends at the local medical research center, I had attracted an impromptu seminar of a dozen different specialists, each one of them more eager than the last to back up the male obsolescence argument. To each researcher, I posed the same questions: "What makes a male what he is? What do you plan to do about it? And why?"

A pair of embryologists with a strong feminist bias gave me the eerie news about what little boys are made of. They loaned me their copy of a marvelous book, Laurel Holliday's *The Violent Sex*, a meticulously researched diatribe against the inherent defects of male psychobiology.

Then three anthropologists discussed aggression and male sex hormones, which brought up the whole horrid business of chemical demasculation. And by this time, the future of the human male was fast becoming an unfunny question. Will we find out about our own demise before we read it in the newspapers?

From the perspective of the endocrine investigator, maleness is the result of a specific sequence of prenatal molecular reactions that can be manipulated with the proper chemical technology. To the psychologist and sociologist, maleness is a matter of roles, attitudes, rituals and myths, all of which are susceptible to another variety of manipulation. A growing faction of social scientists who are studying the nature of human aggession sees world-threatening implications in characteristically "male behavior"—such as war.

We all suspected that Western science and human nature would collide one day, but who could have predicted that the issue of masculinity would furnish the meeting ground? The action on this front flows through several levels, from the molecular to the social, from a few crucial sex hormones to the whole steaming, scheming, furiously humping human mass. Considering what we might gain or lose in the future-shaping game, it would profit any man who values his apparatus to examine the latest facts about how he functions.

The penis, marvel of microengineering that it is, does not

constitute the sole criterion for maleness. An organ is only an organ in the grand biological plan. If your chromosomes want to grow you a new penis or two, who's to say they can't? Who do you think grew it in the first place? The Olympic Committee needs a microscope to tell if certain women athletes are really women athletes because the evolutionary dynamo that makes us rut so much is invisible to the naked eye! Everything needed to make a male and tell him what to do about it is specified by a tiny encoded speck that electron microscopes get lens strain trying to see.

Back where it all began, in the fabled primordial soup, males were not an essential ingredient in the genesis of earthling life. In fact, we didn't come along for quite a while—but when we finally made our appearance, prehistory never knew what hit it.

This comes as a surprise to most men, but here it is: *You started out as a female.* As you may remember from Biology 101, the male-making blueprint is found on the stunted-looking Y chromosome, which only males carry. Although sex is determined at the moment of conception, by the presence or absence of Mister Y in the victorious spermatazoan, there are *no* differences in male and female anatomy until the eighth week of gestation. Up until that point, all human embryos are sexually bipotential, with *identical* external genitalia.

After the critical seventh week, the male fetus jazzes itself with a hot shot of male hormones, called androgens, and the genital tubercle grows into a penis. Normally—that is to say, without the hormone blast—the tubercle remains small and becomes a clitoris. Note that the phrase "male hormones" has proven to be deceptive: Both genders share androgens and estrogens; it is the *ratio* between the hormones that makes the difference. Every "normal" male carries enough estrogen in his body to grow breasts, if it weren't for the fact that the androgens in his body suppress that effect; and most women could grow a beard, if it weren't for the hair-suppresive effects of their higher levels of estrogens.

Boys will be boys, say the endocrinologists, because their molecules tell them so. That quick shot of male juice at eight weeks is exactly what little boys are made of, and the implications have caused all manner of heated dispute in scientific ranks. And when the argument spills out of the scientific community into the political arena, better hang on to your gonads, guys. Androgens are where our future forks, and we might as well face it like men.

Anti-male fanatics may have science on their side when they get around to technological tinkering with the nature of the human male. A number of researchers have proposed that these same androgens that shape our sexual anatomy may also stimulate aggressive behavior in later life. And aggression, though it got us where we are today, sure won't get us there tomorrow. When the tools of the survival trade were fang and claw, our ancestors harnessed their swelling brains and unemployed hands to their aggressive hormones, picked up a few sticks and stones, and beat the hell out of the competition. This took place a few hundred thousand years ago, a mere piffle in evolutionary time, and we may still be burdened by deeply imprinted remnants of bloodlust, which are suicidally inappropriate now that our sticks and stones are thermonuclear.

The revolutionary theory which may affect all credential-carrying males connects the level of male sex hormones in the blood with our tendency to wail on each other. Debate over this question, and research into its validity, continue as you read these words.

If maleness as our hunter-gatherer ancestors defined it is still with us, and if it is proved to be an obstacle to the preservation of civilization, and if we stumble upon the powers to change that factor, will the survival of the species *demand* that we alter the biology of manhood? When that question is raised, it would be handy for the potential alterees to have an answer.

An intriguing theory that is gaining credence would have us pay closer attention to the lower primates for clues to modern social behavior. While there is justifiable criticism from many quarters about the dangers of projecting animal findings onto human actions, there is still an aggressive trick or two we urban-jungle dwellers share with our hairier cousins.

Dominance hierarchies, for example, are said to be a group-survival strategy in many nonhuman primates. The term is the scientific equivalent of the more well-known phrase: "pecking order." In many primates, instead of pecking one another, the males mount one another, briefly and symbolically. That way, every male only has to fight with every other male once, instead of all the time. The one who mounts everyone else and is mounted by no one else gets the first pick of eligible females. By arranging circumstances so that the strongest males get first chance to mate, the dominance hierarchy order ensures that the species will continue to breed aggressive males.

By establishing a symbolic power structure, this social mechanism also keeps the males from spending too much time aggressing and too little time breeding. The key finding, as far as humans are concerned, is the connection between each animal's position in the hierarchy and the amount of androgens circulating in his bloodstream. Not only is there a correlation between male hormone level and position in the hierarchy, but researchers have demonstrated that the prize chimp at the top of the heap and the wimpy little specimen on the bottom can be forced to exchange places by castrating one and androgenizing the other.

In a more subtle experiment, low-status males were placed in an artificial society consisting of males they could dominate and females with whom they therefore could copulate at will. After a few days of this treatment, the lucky specimen's androgen levels skyrocket. Return Mr. Meek to his original group, and the odds are good that he'll start kicking ass. Male aggression in humans can't possibly be as tightly coupled to androgens as it is in slightly lower primates, or else virile corporals wouldn't obey scrawny sergeants, and armies would be incapable of perpetrating group aggression, that quintessential human male specialty.

Obviously, humans have developed a means of moderating the violent messages from our blood, but it seems equally obvious that many of the old reflexes persist, mostly in inappropriate situations. We've graduated from animal skins to three-piece suits, but we may still be paying our respects to submerged dominance structures. The question of who screws whom is a matter of potent significance in the marketplace as well as the bedroom. If your boss calls you on the phone and chews you out and you respond by leaning on your subordinate, you are smack-dab in the middle of a contemporary dominance hierarchy.

What does the hypothesis of vestigial dominance hierarchies do to business institutions now that women have begun to move into high positions in the organization charts? So much anti-female sentiment over the ages and across cultures has focused on the females' bondage to their own hormonal cycles. Could it be that male hormone cycles are equally or more enslaving? If positions in the world of male competition are influenced by subtle hormonal shifts we don't consciously recognize, we might see the day when business executives load up on hormones the way some athletes shoot up steroids.

Since it isn't as easy to experiment with castration and huge doses of hormones in human subjects, social scientists use many indirect measures with other species. As technology and new techniques bring increased power to the new field of psychobiology, new knowledge will become available about the sources of human aggression. When studies of the genetic, hormonal, and psychological components of aggression have progressed far enough—perhaps within the next ten years—it won't take an

Amazon despot to bring up the question of maleness versus the viability of the human species.

If human males are shown to carry some innate tendency toward aggression, fetal androgenization—the eighth-week hot shot of hormones that little boys are made of—is one very likely candidate for the way the male brain is imprinted with hostile circuitry. It was suggested to me, off the record, by one of Virginia's biochemist friends that we might someday want to "promote a more peaceful humanity by altering prenatal androgenization or readjusting hormone levels at puberty."

Forceable chemical emasculation? Don't forget that a recent social revolution was triggered by wide-scale chemical alteration of female hormonal cycles via birth-control pills. How will the culture of the twenty-first century look at the question? Force might not be required if the adjustment took place at adolescence. Boys could be given a choice before the onset of puberty: They could collect an attractive bonus by choosing aggression immunization, which would mute their sexual and aggressive drives and prolong their life-span, or they could remain feisty and horny and have the pick of the underserviced female population in the short lifetime allotted them. Armies wouldn't be possible without generals, and nobody old enough to be a general would want to fight a war. A brief, sexy life—or a long, asexual span? That may be the choice our grandsons will have to face.

What if this psychochemotherapy could be reversed? Aggression and sexual desire for males could be turned down for the dangerous years before forty and turned on again later in life. It might not be such a bad idea to get our education and beginning of our life's work accomplished without contending with erotic passion. Sex might have profound advantages when it is saved for a time of life when people can bring the perspective of a lifetime's experience in human relations to this most intimate of relationships.

Biology aside, the present revolution in *attitudes* has already irrevocably changed the age-old image of masculinity. Although the caveman stereotype is still popular in many quarters, a new paradigm for male behavior, a whole spectrum of new definitions of the meaning of "manhood" have become available recently, largely as a result of the woman's liberation movements. Increasingly, women's success at redefining their social role has led to pressure for men to redefine, or at least reexamine, our own roles, as well.

The final solution to the male question could be less than a generation away, unless our sexual future is rerouted. Considering the zero-male alternative, becoming a brave new male might not look so bad a couple of decades from now. A war of images is raging already, with our minds as the battlefield; and the future of the human male at stake. The way in which future scientific discoveries are going to be applied will be determined by our collective picture of the male future, by the most powerful *idea* of what men ought to be.

There are already a few who think a world without men would be the best future for the species. Others wouldn't mind a touch of biochemical engineering to smooth nature's rough edges. I know, because I've met them, and the weight of their evidence is impressive. Some might say that anti-male technology is an intriguing fantasy but hardly anything to add to the overburdened list of worries for contemporary earthlings. On the other hand, this late into the twentieth century, it is hard to believe that anybody can wholly ignore the radical proposals of some tiny splinter political group—especially when those proposals strike deep chords in our nature and play upon our most explosive emotions.

At this critical point in history, there is more than one probable future for masculinity, a whole range of alternative futures. But how long will these opportunities to shape our future remain open? With every year that passes, the choices narrow. Will our heirs be androgynes, androids, supermales, altered males, sensate males—or females? Tomorrow is a multiple-choice test, because the nature of manhood in the next millennium will depend upon decisions made today. It's time to think about your maleness, men, unless you want to see it become a museum exhibit in an androgen-regulated world someday.

Insect Erotica: Why Have Sex at All?

Entomological erotica may sound oxymoronic, but you'll never be the same once you find out what the bugs already know. Who started the rumor that humans are kinky? It simply isn't true. We're flexible, perverse, and (mostly) imaginative, but we are definitely not kinky. Insects are another story; as a matter of fact, some of our creeping and crawling brethren are *very* bent. Sniff around the scientific literature and you'll discover what I mean.

Tiptoe through the intricacies of arachnid foreplay, and I promise you'll come out of it feeling *normal*, no matter what weird zone you thought you inhabited before you happened onto this page. In fact, if you are easily depressed, you better skip to the next excursion, because these sick little stories might lead you to contemplate a subject you probably don't want to think about. Ultimately, the question of why any self-respecting creature would behave as strangely as the tiny weirdos we are about to meet leads to one of today's hottest scientific questions: Why have sex at all, evolutionarily speaking?

We'll start out easy, because this kind of information can be a shock to the system if you get to the real action too quickly.

Tarantulas are a good place to begin. In one subspecies, the female tarantula is much larger than the male. Big enough to eat his head in one bite, if she is so inclined. Modern science doesn't know whether female tarantulas are mean as hell or whether there is something temptingly tasty about male tarantulas or whether they both know something we don't know, but it has been verified and documented that the female tarantula, upon seeing the male, invariably tries to bite his head off. She often succeeds. The male, a tiny fellow, probably would regard the mating experience with some trepidation if he had enough brain matter to regard anything at all. For humans, the experience might be akin to lobotomized copulation with a five-story-high trash masher.

Fortunately for the subspecies in question, the male tarantula has spurs on his elbows. This anatomical peculiarity, trivial though it might seem, plays a vital role in the closing scenes of *Tarantula Love*. In order to mate, the male tarantula must accomplish several bizarre acts in the biologically proper order. First, he masturbates in his own mouth. Then he approaches his chosen partner. When she opens her jaws to bite his head off, the male sticks his elbows in her mouth and holds it open with his little spurs. He then spits into her mouth. Once the whole memorable act is consummated, it is up to the male to get his spurs unhooked and his thorax moving down the road before his mate succeeds in swallowing him. Most of the men don't make it, but that's the glory of insect love.

Or consider the cephalopods. They aren't insects, but I think you'll agree that they *are* weird. Like the tarantula, the male squid first masturbates. Then, taking a particular kind of seaweed in his tentacles, he rolls his "load" into a cigar, and using a special tentacle (known as the sexual palp), passes it to the object of his affection. The lady squid knows what to do with the "cigar" (but it doesn't sound like a whole lotta fun . . . which leads one to wonder what constitutes sexual deviation for squids—a tiparillo?).

Despite a spectacular performance by the aforementioned wooly arachnids, you really have to hand it to the praying mantis for sheer bizarre sado-necrophilia. The brutal fact is that the female slowly nibbles the head of the male while they hump away in graceful, triple-jointed articulations. With his entire brain eaten away, the male's body continues to pump methodically for hours afterward. The male is physiologically incapable of ejaculation until a certain bothersome lobe of his miniscule brain is removed. Indeed, the presence of a brain seems to inhibit male praying mantis sexuality. In instances like this, it isn't easy to avoid anthropomorphizing the forces of evolution: What could Nature possibly have intended when it cooked up the sexual behavior of the praying mantis?

Black widow spiders earn their name by paralyzing daddy, laying their eggs in his body, then cocooning the whole mess. Dad slowly, slowly dies as the larvae mature; when they hatch, dad becomes hot lunch for the next generation.

Penetration is an important part of sexual behavior in almost every species, but certain insects carry it to extremes. It is certainly nice, speaking from a human male point of view, to place tender parts of my anatomy inside the body of my mate. But I wouldn't want to *live* there, and I don't think I'd want to leave my children there. Or any part of my body. Personally speaking, penetration ought to be a strictly *temporary* arrangement. Try telling that to the male fly of the species *Johannseniella nitida*, who jams his entire body into the female's sperm-storage organ. After completing the act of copulation, the female eats her tightly wedged mate—everything but his sexual organ, which remains locked in place.

I am compelled to digress from the copulatory excesses of the insect world long enough to peek at one of the most eerily perverse fish to flip a fin in God's green ocean. The male anglerfish doesn't die for the pleasure of intercourse with his chosen mate, but he does surrender his freedom as an autonomous creature. The whole anglerfish story could be a soap opera in itself. Like the tarantula, the male anglerfish is an order of magnitude smaller than the female, but that isn't his key characteristic. The weird hand that life deals to a male anglerfish is a tendency for his teeth to fall out early in life, which means he is no longer able to eat for himself. His teeth are replaced by a feeble kind of pincer that doesn't serve any purpose in the fish-eat-fish world he inhabits. In one of those freaky evolutionary counterbalances, however, the male anglerfish, although toothless in the prime of life, has extremely large *nostrils*—large enough to make up a quarter of its head volume.

What can a creature do with gargantuan nostrils? Find pheromones, of course. Which means that the toothless male anglerfish, who literally does not know where his next meal is coming from or how he would eat it if it arrived and plopped itself down in front of him, has one overwhelmingly well-developed talent: He is a sophisticated tracking device, capable of finding female anglerfish in a pinch. As you can imagine, the male is motivated with a sense of urgency to do *something* soon. When he tracks down a female, the male finds himself latching onto the closest part of her body with his new pincers. A biochemically unique transformation occurs where their flesh meets and the two bodies fuse to share the circulatory system of the (much larger) female, which provides nourishment, sometimes to three or four parasitic males at a time. When the female feels like ejecting her eggs into the water, the parastic males eject their sperm. Once it is parasitized the only function of the male anglerfish's body is to fertilize eggs when the female gets the urge. After a while, the male's tiny body shrivels even further, until it is little more than a container for testes, clinging wart-like to the female's skin.

The sex life of the male dungbeetle is less heavily dependent than that of the anglerfish, but some might consider it to be even more humiliating. In a touching mating ritual, the male dung beetle scuttles about the environment, collects bits and pieces of fecal matter, rolling them into a roughly spherical object as he goes. When the shitball gets big enough, he presents it to the female for approval. At times, popular females are literally surrounded by a moving wall of dung, as their many prospective suitors move in on them from all directions. When the female signals her approval of one particular offering, she and her chosen mate roll the ball of dung together, dragging it through the entrance of her den. Then they get romantic in whatever room is still unoccupied by dung. Sounds strange, you say? Not for six-legged critters. The practice of food offerings is common through the insect world, and shitballs are not all that rare.

In other species, sex can be a literally explosive affair. A male honeybee selected by the queen for a royal dalliance consummates his sex life and the rest of his life at the same time, when his genitals explode within the queen's body. She goes on to live the life of a queen—that is, as a pampered egg-laying machine—and he doesn't go on to anything.

In the world of bristle worms, however, the male isn't the one who faces an irreversible sexual fate. While they are mating, the male wraps himself around the female. She bites him, which causes him to release his sperm, which she swallows. In a few seconds, the sperm travels through her digestive track to her eggs, fertilizes them, then causes the female bristle worm's abdomen to explode, thus broadcasting the eggs into the environment.

What is going on here? What is all this weird fuss about? These are questions that evolutionary biologists and sociobiologists are actively investigating and debating. The proliferation of bizarre mating strategies and counterstrategies in so many species, including the elaborate role-playing of primates (including the hairless kind), has been cited as evidence for sociobiology's claim that mating behavior is a market economy where the payoff in the mating game for any individual is measured in terms of how many of his or her genes are propagated into future generations. But the question still remains: Why is *sexual* reproduction so successful? Why have sex at all?

The conventional wisdom has been that sexual exchange of genetic material from two parents is ubiquitous in nature because it is a powerful means of producing genetically diverse offspring. In the evolutionary scenario, environmental factors (including predators that feed on young things) meet up with genetic factors (number of offspring, range of diversity among offspring), and determine the payoff. The more gene carriers you put into a hostile environment, the greater their chances of survival; and when your offspring differ from one another while still carrying your genes, you raise the probability that those genes will be propagated into many different niches in the ecosystem. New theories have questioned the mainstream view, directing attention to the enormous costs in energy, time, and attention that individuals must pay for participating in sex. In that tradeoff, is diversity really so advantageous that so many species go to so much trouble for a hot date on Saturday night?

In an article in *The New York Times* ("Why Sex Baffles Biologists," April 24, 1986), reporter Erik Eckholm, writing about the new biological theories regarding the origins and prevalence of sexual reproduction, noted: "None of these new theories is flattering to males of any species. At best, males are portrayed as useful sources of genetic diversity. One theory justifies males as storehouses of redundant information that females can draw on, if necessary, to repair damaged genes. Another describes sex as a sort of disease, with males mere agents of contagion."

The male-as-spare-parts-warehouse theory was espoused by Richard Michod and four of his colleagues at the University of Arizona. Their reasoning is seductive, if unflattering to the male ego. Think of genes as blueprints in the form of telegrams to the future. The blueprints contain the evolved informational wisdom on how to make a rhinoceros or a protozoan look or act the way rhinoceri or protozoa act. In the grand competitive scheme of things, all the blueprint-specified details from how the individual cells synthesize proteins to the way males strut around during mating season can directly affect how successfully individual organisms fare in the environment. The blueprints are encoded in the arrangement of molecules in the DNA strands that are coiled within the chromosomes of the sex cells of each organism of the species. When the organism reproduces, the blueprints are copied and thus "telegraphed" into the future, via the chromosomes of the offspring. The problem with this scheme is that the messages tend to get garbled over time, especially over long periods of time, something like the way images deteriorate on office copiers when you make a copy of a copy of a copy.

These garbled messages, known as "transcription errors" because the reproduction process involves a kind of transcription of the older generation's DNA into the younger generation's chromosomes, can be caused by solar radiation, natural chemicals in the environment, or viruses and are irreversible in the sense that there aren't any natural agents that turn garbled messages back into their original correct versions. That's where sex and males come in. "Males are a way of providing redundant information," Michod told the Times reporter: "When females are damaged, they can use information from males to repair their bad genes." If your first offspring hops instead of slithers, just find a new father, who has an intact slithering gene. Keep males around and keep them interested, and you have a handy pool of undamaged genes. Of course, by this hypothesis, once molecular biologists come up with a synthetic gene-repair mechanism, males technically become obsolete.

The males-as-infection hypothesis was proposed by Michael Rose and Donal Hickey, two Canadian scientists, who question whether sexual reproduction conveys any evolutionary benefit! It's just a very, very, successful infection! They point to the recent discovery of "plasmids," which are DNA sequences, similar to viruses, that reproduce by injecting themselves into the reproductive cells of other organisms, staying there without harming the host organism, and going along for the ride, thus spreading through populations of cells and organisms. In the world of bacteria, some of these free-lance DNA sequences actively seek and infect new kinds of cells. Rose and Hickey propose that sexual reproduction might have developed as a way of insuring the spread of these evolutionary hitch-hikers! The evolutionary benefits of sexual reproduction, under this theory, would have come into play only after this parasitic relationship became prevalent throughout the global gene pool.

Are we spare parts, men? Or are we an infection? To some, these might seem like academic questions that only specialists in white coats might care about. It is worth noting, however, that changes in basic scientific knowledge can lead to profound and widespread changes in the way most of the people in the world lead their lives. The Copernican Revolution led to the scientific, technological, and industrial revolutions that created the modern world. The theory of evolution irrevocably changed our notions of what human beings are, where we came from, and where we are headed. The effects of new discoveries relating to the biological origins of sex promise to be no less profound and far-reaching. Those torrid tarantulas and kinky cuttlefish might be trying to tell us something about ourselves.

The Shape of the Universe

It can, however, also come about, if I have both will and grace, that in considering the tree I become bound up in relation to it.

Martin Buber

The shape of the universe is right there in front of you, if nobody has chopped it down yet. If you are fortunate enough to have a leafy elm, a gnarly oak, a soaring redwood in your neighborhood, make a point of looking at it soon, for the recursive silhouette of a tree against the sky is more than a poetic image. It's a clue to several cosmic riddles and a key concept in fields as unrelated as vascular surgery and software design.

The Buddha knew this, and so does every self-respecting neurologist, mathematician, mythologist, and chess player.

The Buddha, an aristocratic truth seeker from that part of the world now known as Nepal, achieved a state of perfect, unexcelled enlightenment while sitting under a tree in Northern India, early one morning 2,500 years ago. Libraries of commentaries in dozens of languages have analyzed the significance of the state of mind attained by that seeker in that place and moment. Legions of metaphysicians have debated the various methods of achieving the same state of mind. Less well known, especially in the Western world, has been the ancient and curious history of the *tree* under whose protection the noetic breakthrough occurred.

It stands out like a ponderosa on a prairie once you pay attention to it: The tree is a ubiquitous symbol in a universal religious story that was at least five hundred years old by the time of Jesus. *Axis mundi*, the axis of the world, is the tree at the center of everything sacred. Mythologist Joseph Campbell, referring to the Buddha's tree-shaded awakening, noted that: "This is the most important single moment in Oriental mythology, a counterpart of the Crucifixion of the West. The Buddha beneath the Tree of Enlightenment (the Bo Tree) and Christ on Holy Rood (the Tree of Redemption) are analogous figures, incorporating an archetypal World Savior, World Tree motif, which is of immemorial antiquity."[1]

Hindu mythology, which was already ancient in Buddha's time, used the tree for metaphors of the inner self: The yogic map of the "spirit body" shows a metaphysical physiology that is rooted in the base of the spine and rises up through a series of energy centers along the ascending shaft of the spine, culminating in a thousand-petalled lotus. When the yogi succeeds in raising the Kundalini, he achieves a state of mind that sounds like a very close relative of Buddha's satori, known as *Nirvikalpa Samadhi*, which means more or less the same thing: "complete, unexcelled enlightenment."

The upside-down tree also figures in Hindu dream mythology. The key to Hindu dream myths is the understanding that dreams and waking are metaphors for the illusion of waking life and the greater Awakening that can happen when awareness works its way to the top of the tree. To Hindu dream adepts, the question of *how do you know that you are awake* is one that applies to waking as well as dreaming. David Shulman, in *Tamil Temple Myths,* discussing a character in a myth who realizes that he is actually dreaming the tragedy of his life, notes: "The nature of his delusion is clear from the moment he first catches sight of the upside-down tree—a classic Indian symbol for the reality that underlies and is hidden by life in the world, with its false goals and misleading perceptions." The Indian Rope Trick of Kipling stories, tourist entertainments, and B movies, in which a fakir makes a rope stand on end, climbs up the rope, and disappears, is a pop-culture theatrical metaphor for the same hidden message.

To say nothing of the Garden of Eden. When you start looking for it, tree symbology turns up everywhere. Why do trees always happen to be on the set when God talks? It doesn't matter whether your cosmology is Hebraic or Christian, Hindu, Buddhist, Pagan, or Animist: Trees are always part of the scenery whenever a theophany happens. Just because trees don't have a speaking role, worshippers of every stripe have assumed that the trees in these world-transforming scenes serve simply as mute background to the dialogue between humans and the divine. In some of the oldest known religions, however, the true story is quite the reverse. The World-Tree, *Ygdrassill, Axis Mundi,* the Tree of Knowledge are the reality in these arboreal theologies, and the human-divine dialogue is the illusion.

It simply wouldn't have been the same kind of unexcelled perfect enlightenment if Buddha had been sitting under a waterfall or a neon sign, but few people seem to have been interested in the spiritual significance of the *Bodhi* ("enlightenment") tree. This much is known: The Buddha's tree was the type now known as pipal (*ficus religiosa*), and it was precisely as old as the fellow who sat down in its shade to catch a case of satori. Legend maintains that it was no accident that the Enlightened One sat under that particular tree at that specific time: Sakyamuni, as he was known before he Woke Up, had a lifelong habit of sitting under pipal trees that were exactly as old as him. It is also said, in Sanskrit circles, that Buddha's mother (aka Maya devi) held onto the branches of a pipal when she gave birth to the Enlightened-One-to-be. (This tree-grasping birth pose is important enough to rate its own Sanskrit name: *salabhanjika pose*.) If you think enlightenment must be an intense sensation, think about the act of giving birth to the Enlightened One.

Why a tree? Why not a seashell, a lightning bolt, an old man with a beard? The iconography is not strictly Asian. Indeed, the theme surfaces in folk tales, holy books, cave paintings, tiled mosques, and frescoed chapels in every part of the globe. The Chinese saw it as a giant peach tree that bears the fruit of immortality. Every year, as the winter solstice approaches, hundreds of millions of Christians place a symbolic pine tree in their houses and cover it with ornaments. The Yule log dates back to Druid and Celtic customs of pre-Christian Britain, which at one time was covered in dense forests. The custom of the Christmas tree originated in Germany, where it also appears that people were treating trees as sacred beings long before the birth of Jesus. In the nineteenth century, German scholars discovered that the word *temple* is derived from the Indo-European roots for *sacred grove*.

This symbol, found everywhere and in every era, represents the universe as a living organism, a map that serves equally well for the cosmos external to the individual and the spectrum of consciousness deep within—with its highest branches in the heavens and its roots deep within the dark underrealm. Before God the Father, even before the Goddess, did a much older faith flourish, one that goes back beyond our prehistoric ancestry, all the way to our origins as a species?

Tree worship in its pure form has not died out but has become for the most part the realm of the poet now, rather than the prophet. The Bengali poet Tagore, speaking from a tradition of arboreal reverence that has been alive and well on the Indian subcontinent for millennia, wrote this ode-prayer:

Oh tree, you are the *adi-prana*, the primal source of life. You were the first to hear the call of the sun and to liberate life from the prisonhouse of the rock. You represent the first awakening of consciousness. You brought to the earth beauty and peace. Before you came, the earth was dumb; you filled her breath with music.

Are we drawn to trees because our minds know that our brains are shaped like them? Do these signatures of our internal informational structure keep emerging in symbols of our deepest religious impulses because they are what nineteenth-century anthropologist Adolf Bastian called *Elementargedanken*—"elementary ideas" that are hardwired into our brains? C.G. Jung called them archetypes and pointed out that they are wired to the cosmos as well as our psyches. As any Jungian therapist will tell you, religious symbols are often messages from our collective unconscious about things we ought to know, even if we can't put that knowledge into words. We're trying to tell ourselves something.

Some of the tree-things we know are as metaphysical as you can get; others are downright quantifiable. For one thing, time is a tree and we've always known it. Each one of the Many Worlds is just a leaf on an infinitely branching tree of alternate futures. For another thing, our nervous systems are shaped like trees, and so are rivers, capillaries, data structures, probability worlds, solution-spaces, chess games, and chain reactions. We used to live in them. It's no wonder that Buddhas-elect decide to sit under them when they are ready to Awaken.

One characteristic that doesn't vary much from one tree to another is the way smaller parts of the tree, the larger and smaller branches and twigs, reflect the shape of the entire tree; a computer programmer would recognize the tree as a "recursive structure" (because the same pattern "recurs" at both the top and bottom levels of organization). This shape is the reason trees and other things look treelike, and the concept furnishes a crucial clue to several important questions in science and technology: What is the most efficient way to organize complex systems? How can you keep track of a billion units of anything and make sure you can find each unit as quickly as possible? How do you move many things from one point to many other points by the shortest routes? A recursive, branching tree shape is the visual symbol for the answer to all these questions.

The tree shape is familiar even to people who live near floodplains instead of forests, because trees are not the only phenomena to adopt this form for reasons of efficiency. Indeed, branching structures are clearly one of the fundamental shapes in the universe. Not only the metaphysical worlds of religious symbols and psychological archetypes, but the natural world of trees and rivers and arteries and the artificial worlds of mathematical and logic and computer memories are filled with branching things. A tree of the botanical variety is shaped the way it is because branching is the most efficient way to collect moisture from the earth and distribute it to a hundred thousand leaves. (And since esoteric traditions like Kabbalism envision the path to God-consciousness as a tree shape, is a recursively branching path also the most efficient way to distribute consciousness to numberless sentient beings, to emanate God-ness throughout creation?)

Examine an aerial photograph of a river delta next to an X-ray arteriogram of a human lung and you'll see that branches aren't limited to forests. This similarity of form in very different natural systems is no accident. Rivers branch as they run into their own sedimentary deposits because an arboreal shape is the most efficient way to distribute the river's flow when the main channel suddenly becomes shallow. Pulmonary arteries branch because that enables the lungs to distribute oxygen to the blood rapidly. The branching of nerves and blood vessels in the brain is known technically as "arborization."

Quantum physicists even dreamed up fourth-dimensional trees, back when the "many worlds interpretation" surfaced. Because of certain essential aspects of the equations describing the transformations of electromagnetic energy, first formulated at the beginning of the twentieth century, it is possible to hypothesize that the universe is an infinitely branching entity. This is not just metaphysical speculation, but a formally permissible (if as-yet-unconfirmed) consequence of the quantum equations. It is known formally as The Copenhagen Interpretation of Quantum Physics, or informally as The Many-Worlds Hypothesis. It's one of those rare scientific theories that makes intuitive sense to everybody because everybody has wondered, at one time or another, about the roads not taken in their past and the futures that might have been. Every moment that you or I experience is fraught with infinite possibilities, but only one of those possibilities is actualized at any one moment. Sooner or later, the same crazy thought intrudes into just about everybody's mind: "What if all those roads not taken, those concatenating worlds of if, do exist in some multiple parallel dimensions?"

Your lifeline and mine—our paths through time, known formally by quantum physicists as our "worldlines"—branch when we make decisions, take action, hesitate, move, or stand still. There are worlds in which you are the Buddha (and Buddhist eschatology agrees with this corollary) and worlds that are exactly the same as this one, except you part your hair on the opposite side. Although it isn't easy to visualize, the abstract space of such a universe, filled with infinities of nonintersecting branches, is a fourth-dimensional tree that grows at a rate incomprehensible to a three-dimensional mindset. It would be like explaining an expanding balloon in three-space to a flatlander—an inhabitant of a two-dimensional plane who can never get beyond the idea of a circle.

A tree can be a map of time, or it can be a map of information. Tree-shaped data structures are essential parts of all computer software systems at both the lowest and the highest levels, because trees are such an efficient way to store and retrieve large amounts of ordered information. Trees also reflect the shape of binary codes, and that puts them very close to the roots of computation. A tree in which each node branches into exactly two more branches is the direct visual analog of a binary code, because you can get from the trunk to any one of the leaves by making either one of two decisions at each branch (e.g., take either the left branch or the right branch at each successive node, starting from the trunk and ending at the specified leaf).

If you were compulsive enough, you could assign a unique address to each leaf on a tree by specifying the binary decisions that a bug would have to make to travel directly from the trunk to that leaf. You could, for example, specify the leaf on the first right branch after the first left branching of the right fork of the main trunk and call it right-left-right (or, for brevity, r-l-r or, for that matter, 010 or 101). This scheme might be helpful to people in cities, as well as to bugs on trees: For example, we can apply the same analogy to the problem of explaining how to find a certain location in a city to a newcomer who can count but can't read street signs: "Take your first right, go two blocks, turn left for one block," and so on.

When you begin attaching instructions to a binary-branching structure, as in the case of the instruction-literate bug or the illiterate traveler, you actually are describing the basis of computer software, the fundamental alphabet and grammar of every computer language. Niklaus Wirth, one of the high theoreticians of computer science, has decreed that all computer programs consist of only two things: algorithms and data structures. Algorithms are lists of instructions for machines to follow. Data structures are linguistic shapes for information that humans create for use by machines, formalized ways to encode problems and data for the algorithms to process. Choosing appropriate data structures is an essential element of programming because it doesn't matter how elegantly your algorithms can crunch numbers if your data structures require you to crunch them for a hundred years.

An AI programmer once told me that tree-shaped data structures are "a way to fan out quickly into a solution space." If you were crazy enough to build a brute-force machine for playing chess—one that evaluated every possible move and chose the best one at every turn—you would find yourself caught in an exploding number tree. Not even all the supercomputers in the world would be able to keep up with this task after a few moves. You simply can't get very far into any chess game without the number of possible moves to evaluate growing larger than the number of atoms in the universe. Watch out for any procedure that starts with a small ante and then makes you repeat it for every branch of a recursively branching structure. It was Claude Shannon, the father of information theory, who demonstrated that the brute-force method was not a viable approach to a chess-playing program. In his article, he showed how the explosively branching tree is destined to destroy any brute-force approach after only a few steps.

There are ways to prune data-trees so they don't grow out of control, however, and when the first computer jockeys started talking about artificial intelligence in the 1950s, they thought tree-shaped searches through problem space were the way to go. In the 1980s, the art and science of cultivating tree-shaped data structures is still on the forefront of software technology and AI research. "Forward-chaining logic," one of the new buzzwords in the subfield of expert systems, uses a modified tree structure. And binary-tree search procedures are on the very forefront of computer science. Like the quest for the ultimate particle that has taken possession of physics, the quest for the ultimate tree has become a similar obsession in some rarefied quarters of knowledge engineers and AI language designers.

The nicest thing about trees is the way the trees themselves seem to cut right through all the abstractions and multidisciplinary analyses: No matter what your specialty, it is virtually certain that you have had at least one personal friend in your lifetime who happened to be a tree. Kids know about trees. They climb them, lie down under them, hang swings from them, build treehouses in them, paint pictures of them, collect their leaves. It is possible to have a relationship with a tree. Nobody has ever stated this better than Martin Buber, in one of the first stanzas of his spiritual classic, *I and Thou:*

> I consider a tree.
>
> I can look on it as a picture: stiff column in a shock of light, or splash of green shot with the delicate blue and silver of the background.
>
> I can perceive it as movement: flowing veins on clinging, pressing pith, suck of the roots, breathing of the leaves, ceaseless commerce with earth and air—and the obscure growth itself.
>
> I can classify it in a species and study it as a type in its structure and mode of life.
>
> I can subdue its actual presence and form so sternly that I recognise it only as an expression of law—of the laws in accordance with which a constant opposition of forces is continually adjusted, or of those in accordance with which the component substances mingle and separate.
>
> I can dissipate it and perpetuate it in number, in pure numerical relation.
>
> In all this the tree remains my object, occupies space and time, and has its nature and constitution.
>
> It can, however, also come about, if I have both will and grace, that in considering the tree I become bound up in relation to it. The tree is now no longer *It.* I have been seized by the power of exclusiveness.
>
> To effect this it is not necessary for me to give up any of the ways in which I consider a tree. There is nothing from which I would have to turn my eyes away in order to see, and no knowledge that I would have to forget. Rather is everything, picture and movement, species and type, law and number, indivisibly united in this event.[2]

Trees are talismans of sanity and wholeness. Post-Jungian depth psychologists and straightforward clinical psychologists agree on this. An entire battery of projective tests that are in widespread clinical use, known as the "House-Person-Tree" technique, is based on the systematic interpretation of drawings people make of these three significant components of every person's personal environment. According to Jungians, the appearance of a tree as a symbol in a dream can be most fortuitous, in the sense that it symbolizes, empowers, and heralds a movement toward wholeness of the personality. Marie-Louise von Franz notes that: "Since . . . psychic growth cannot be brought about by a conscious effort of will power, but happens involuntarily and naturally, it is in dreams frequently symbolized by the tree, whose slow, powerful involuntary growth fulfills a definite pattern."

Although the significance of those forces symbolized by the World-Tree has not diminished, the chance of the average earthling having physical contact or spiritual relationships with trees has diminished dramatically. The Cedars of Lebanon were deforested since the days when they were mentioned in the Old Testament. The Sahara was once a forest, before people started pulling it down—without the assistance of modern technology. And the first energy crisis in Europe occurred when the great forests were cut down for firewood and people had to turn to coal as an energy source. Deforestation is now one of the most serious ecological challenges facing the planet. An important aspect of the entire planet's life-support system—the exchange of carbon dioxide for oxygen in the atmosphere—has, until now, been regulated by the world's forests and the ocean's plankton. Within a few decades, we will have eliminated the forests. Presumably, someone is cooking up a way to destroy the plankton.

Quite simply stated, the human species is in the process of removing all the trees on the planet, except for a few small preserves, by the end of this century. Increasingly wealthy multinational corporations do it for profit. Growing numbers of peasants do it to stay warm at night. The consequences might be dire for the human race. They are certainly disastrous for millions of species that will never walk, slither, or fly above the earth again. In the words of biologist Daniel Simberloff:

> Tropical forests are being besieged by armies of subsistence farmers who cannot survive in cities. . . . Each year humans destroy enough tropical forest to blanket all of England. Among the several dire implications of this devastation is that a mass extinction of tropical species appears imminent. And, since tropical forests are the homes of between two and four million of the estimated five to ten million species on the face of the earth, it could well rank with history's several great mass extinctions.[3]

The fate of our grandchildren depends on the fate of the trees in ways we can't suspect. Out there in those ten million species are powerful anticancer drugs and an unknowable quantity of other potentially life-saving knowledge. Out there are ten million experiments, ten million essential organs of the planetary hivemind that took billions of years to develop, but which are being destroyed in less than a hundred years. We'll never know what we're missing until the whole shebang becomes uninhabitable. In a sense, those of us alive today are like the population of China that was alive at the time the emperor ordered all previous knowledge to be destroyed, all books to be burned. Because of that man's actions over a few years, every bit of knowledge and wisdom that had been written by previous scholars for centuries is lost to posterity. Another biologist, Edward O. Wilson, puts it this way:

> . . . if no country pulls the [nuclear] trigger the worst thing that will *probably* happen—in fact is already well underway—is not energy depletion, economic collapse, conventional war, or even the expansion of totalitarian governments. As tragic as these catastrophes would be for us, they can be repaired within a few generations. The one process now going on that will take millions of years to correct is the loss of genetic and species diversity by the destruction

of natural habitats. This is the folly our descendants are least likely to forgive us.[4]

Which means that the act of planting a tree has taken on profound ecological as well as psychological and spiritual significance. I believe there is a pathway to a response to the global tree problematique, and that we can learn something of value by widely adopting the Bantu word *mahamba*, which refers to the spirit-tree that is planted when a child is born. The clear passage to a solution: Make tree-planting a sacred act again. The place to start is by planting a new word in our language, a new meme in our cultural group-mind.

The importance of *mahamba* planting is rivalled only by its simplicity: As soon as possible after you or your wife or a relative or a close friend gives birth, take the child and its parents out to plant a *mahamba*. Make sure that the tree is of a variety native to the environment, that it has a chance of survival, and that it will be accessible in the future. Finding a proper place to plant and obtaining an appropriate seedling might not be an easy task; this difficulty is the spiritual offering of the child's sponsor. As soon as the child is able to walk, bring him or her out to meet the tree and to feed it. Encourage the child to take over the care and feeding and keep reinforcing the merit to be gained from the act in whatever terms the child understands: Like Santa Claus, the legend of a tree that brings you good fortune might be one of those harmless myths that can teach a child more than a hundred hard facts. And the simple act of nurturing a tree, distributed memetically, repeated recursively, might be the only way for our species to get a grip on our runaway throttle.

PART 3

COGNITIVE TECHNOLOGIES

Future Highs

4 IX 2039. *I finally learned how to come into possession of an encyclopedia. I already own one now—the whole thing contained in three glass vials. Bought them in a science psychedeli. Books are no longer read but eaten, not made of paper but of some informational substance, fully digestible, sugar-coated. I also did a little browsing in a psychem supermarket. Self-service. Arranged on the shelves are beautifully packaged low-calorie opinionates, gullibloons—credibility beans?—abstract extract in antique gallon jugs, and iffies, argumunchies, puritands and dysecstasy chips. . . . At first I was skeptical, but accepted this innovation when after taking four algebrine capsules I suddenly found myself perfectly at home in higher mathematics. . . . Friends are not an indispensable source of information; you can take a drug called duetine which doubles your consciousness in such a way that you can hold discussions with yourself on any topic. . . .*

—Stanislaw Lem, *The Futurological Congress*

111

By the year 2001, will the man and woman above town select their states of consciousness from moment to moment and commute between mental levels as easily as we now commute between continents? What kind of world would we be living in today if the psychedelic experimentation of the 1960s had led to a full-scale science of consciousness, instead of triggering, as it did, an only partially successful social revolution that degenerated into an era of recreational drug abuse? Is it possible that the science and technology of mind-expansion might outgrow the legal and social taboos of the 1980s to carry the quest for consciousness into the vast realm opened up for us when Albert Hoffman accidentally embarked on the world's first acid trip?

To Stanislaw Lem, the author of the passage quoted above, the "cryptochemocracy" of the future was a science-fiction plot. And so were moon rockets, to Jules Verne. The foundations of that weird new world of tomorrow are being constructed today, by scientists, not science-fiction writers: While drug designers modernize the ancient art of intoxication, social scientists are sketching scenarios about the future of our mental state. Note that I'm not talking about drug abuse. The difference between drug abuse and psychochemical exploration is akin to the difference between mayhem and neurosurgery.

Less well known than the smugglers and mindblowers of the media age have been the serious explorers of interior space who mapped a few of the tricky dimensions beyond the normal spectrum of consciousness long before the invention of the phrase "recreational drug abuse." A few of them are still at work. Some seeker of inner knowledge may be risking life, limb, and brain damage while you read this, just to bring you a better way to alter your consciousness. At this moment, anthropologists in the Amazon are searching for telepathy-inducing vines, and chemists in New Jersey are hallucinating the shapes of their next molecular euphoriants. Transpersonal psychotherapists are known to be floating in tanks of salt water and psychophysiologists have been seen tuning their nervous systems to new resonant frequencies via microelectronic yoga.

The more sensational protagonists of the psychedelic era long ago left the orbit of orthodox science. But the study of consciousness expansion has remained very much alive. The inner-space experts of the eighties are wary of publicity. But turned-on scientists do exist. John Lilly, the former dolphin researcher and inventor of the flotation tank, chronicled his exploration of sensory deprivation combined with various drugs from the first legal LSD provided by the United States Institutes of Mental Health to little-known "dissociative" drugs like ketamine; Michael Harner, the anthropologist-shaman, who uses drumming, chanting, and visualization to open the door to the other worlds; Jean Houston, the "how-to" guru of the neo-psychedelic revolution, and others. Then there's G., who might be the dignified gentleman in front of you in the supermarket line, who has devoted his career to the chemical pursuit of higher planes of mind.

Somewhere in America dwells a quiet man who is the very image of the eminent scientist. He is respected in his field, but due to the taboos surrounding his specialty, he wishes to remain anonymous. He doesn't even want to disclose what part of the country he lives in. Dr. G., as I agreed to call him, synthesizes substances that have never before existed on this planet, mind-benders of such complexity that an evolved consciousness is required to even imagine their structures.

Like any technology, the first products of psychochemistry have been crude "uppers" or "downers" or "tranquillizers." Eventually, more subtle effects will be possible. Will we still eschew chemical mood-changers when they help us think better, or inspire us to create and invent? That is one of the answers G. seeks. It was he who told me about Lem's *Futurological Congress*, a fictional depiction of a future psycho-chemical civilization where hypothetical "benignimizers" like

Hedonidil, Euphoril, Inebrium, Felecitine, Empathan, and, yes, Ecstasine, induced states of undirected joy and beatitude. And, as G. quoted to me toward the beginning of our first talk ". . . by replacing an amino group with a hydroxyl you obtained, instead, Furiol, Antagonil, Rabiditine, Sadistizine . . . and many other polyparanoidal stimulants. . . ." It turns out that G. is closer than Lem might have suspected to a high level of psychosynthetic specificity. By replacing a hydroxy with a methoxy at a certain position on the aromatic ring of one of his compounds, G. has produced a reproducible change in perceptual effects.

Dr. G. was inventing mind-altering drugs decades ago, when everyone still thought LSD was a kind of landing craft. We aren't talking about some kind of bootlegger here, but a genuine, legitimate, licensed pharmaceutical chemist. And if you don't think pharmaceutical chemistry is an important part of our society, consider the fact that several *billion* tranquillizers are consumed this year in the USA alone. The big drug manufacturers have buildings full of pharmaceutical chemists who try to think up new ways to send us up, down, or sideways. G., however, has his sights on tranquillity, insight, joy, inspiration—all those states of mind we traditionally request in prayers to gods or invocations of muses.

It is Dr. G's custom and scientific protocol to ingest his own compounds and commune with the geometry of his transformed perceptions, sometimes finding clues to his next creation in the pattern of his hallucinations. G. considers this deliberate, systematic hallucinating to be a valid tool for using new drugs to create newer drugs. He defends the ethics of this procedure as "the epitome of informed consent," and has published articles in technical journals on the various protocols he uses for self-mapping new mindspaces. There are bound to be some harrowing adventures along the way, like the time he discovered a psychedelic that lasts longer than LSD and took a tenfold overdose. Bizarre as this research method might seem, there is historical precedent for hallucinatory theorizing: The science of organic chemistry was born when a chemist named Kekule dreamed of a snake that swallowed its own tail and awoke to draw the first diagram of the tail-swallowing benzene ring.

Dr. G. is an independent researcher. Employed by no single university, pharmaceutical firm, or government agency, he is welcome at many of them. Our first meeting was in the lounge outside the pharm-chem lab of one of the nation's leading medical schools. Whenever he shows up, he has the run of the place. G. is thoroughly respectable in the eyes of the law and the opinion of the scientific community; indeed, he is admired by his peers. His private laboratory is supported by the royalties from patents he holds for pharmaceuticals that are commercially marketed. If he is going to bring these substances into our world, G. wants to take the responsibility and risk of finding out what they do to a human nervous system. The most important skill, the one that can't be taught, but only *learned*, is how to recognize a molecule's psychoactive effect by imagining its shape.

"Mood-changing drugs can be organized into chemical families," he says, "each with its own qualitative aura. The psychological effect of any drug, including the sense of being high, can be changed by systematically altering its chemical arrangement, especially in those areas we have identified as active sites. A carbon atom here, a free electron there, and you have the difference between insight and anxiety. Some drugs induce fear or a feeling of well-being, others evoke pleasure, distorted or heightened perception, paranoia, or awe. I look for those connections between chemistry and consciousness. Many of the drugs we create in laboratories are analogs, or synthetic reconstructions, of compounds that exist in nature. Other psychopharmaceutical creations never existed until they were synthesized. Both categories hold virtually endless possibilities for exploration. It all depends on how their shapes resemble the shapes of the chemicals in our own brains. Maybe Lem was joking about all the possible states of mind we might find in a pill some day. Maybe he was prophesying."

Dr. G. is in touch with the post-Castaneda generation of anthropologists, who have turned up a psychoactive cornucopia of ritual substances: "The potions of Native American shamans contain many powerful psychoactive drugs that have not been studied under laboratory conditions until recently," G. explains. "There are so many active compounds in each of those snuffs and infusions that it will take years to study them one at a time. We already have a few highly specific derivatives of natural compounds, drugs that are primarily visual, or auditory, or conceptual in their effects . . . but there are usually unpleasant side effects. In the next twenty years, we'll see drugs with every conceivable specific desirable effect, without the undesirable side effects."

Considering the impact of alcohol, tobacco, tranquillizers, heroin, cocaine, and marijuana, there isn't much doubt that psychoactive drugs have a powerful influence on every aspect of our society. But the feeling of benumbed well-being associated with the most commonly abused drugs isn't the only possible drug-induced state. In the early 1980s, word spread quietly through psychotherapeutic circles of a new substance that enabled patients to relax strong inner barriers, eased fears, and in some cases augmented the therapeutic process. MDMA, as this substance was known before some very smart underground entrepreneur dubbed it Ecstasy, became a drug of abuse and was quickly prohibited by law, even for legitimate researchers and therapists. Of this drug, G. said "it shouldn't be considered a hallucinogen. It's more like an empathogen." Perhaps MDMA's successor actually does produce a profound state of empathy with all humankind. Is that so harmful? Suppress your knee-jerk reaction to the idea of solving humankind's problems by pharmaceutical means. Human beings in their sober mode of consciousness aren't exactly paragons of humane behavior. In a world that's armed to the teeth and more, perhaps "benigni-mizers" is just what planet Earth needs.

The psychic powers attributed to sorcerers or supernatural beings in nearly every culture in the world, to cite a different kind of example, might become available through modern rela-tives of the more exotic psychoactive chemicals such as the beta-carbolines and the tryptamines. Time distortion, rebirth experiences, flight of the astral body, extraordinary healings, have been attributed to various visionary chemicals that were unknown to Western science until recently. Harmaline, for ex-ample, was long known as Telepathine, and Dr. G's time-distorter is related to the snuff Columbus saw native Caribs snorting in 1492. Just as quinine and dozens of other potions derived from the world's folk medicines contributed powerful tools to the Western medical pharmacopia, might some as-yet-undiscovered folk knowledge about consciousness-alteration tools hold great promise for Western psychology and psycho-therapy?

One of the major tasks of medical anthropologists in the clos-ing decades of the twentieth century is to find and preserve the pharmaceutical knowledge, quickly disappearing, that is in the possession of the kinds of people we used to call "witch doc-tors," who live in the endangered kinds of societies we used to call "primitive." The next decades will bring a few of these rare shamanistic compounds to light, and eventually they will be recreated in the laboratory. Tragically, many more cultures, and the knowledge they possess, will be extinct by the time we fully appreciate their psychopharmaceutical achievements. Perhaps one of the shamanistic cultures we have been able to study to some degree will show us how to help preserve that natural world before it is bulldozed.

But exotic chemistry isn't the only pathway to a scientifically stoned tomorrow. One promising neo-American mind-altering technique that wasn't borrowed from the natives is the "electronic high." Direct electrical stimulation of the pleasure centers has long been suggested by the extremist brain-abuse fringe as a possible future intoxicant, but until the decadence factor in our society increases beyond the saturation point, few people are likely to drill holes in their heads, insert electrodes in their midbrains, and jolt themselves with volts, just to get high. More subtle and less invasive are electronic techniques, now in their infancy, that might someday enable us to *steer* our minds, with or without chemicals working on our brains.

My friend John Criglar, for example, works with solid-state circuitry rather than with glassware and chemicals, but he is also one of the new cartographers of interior geography. Criglar started out designing radio-telescopes, invented voice-modulated synthesizers for rock groups and experimental telephones for A.T.&T., and was formerly a biomedical engineer at St. Joseph's hospital in San Francisco. His hospital work involved designing and testing a device that monitors muscle relaxation and feeds it back to the patient in the form of audible tones.

When the target muscle is tense, the patient hears one kind of sound; when the muscle relaxes, the pitch of the sound changes. A few electrodes that resemble half-dollar-sized Band-Aids are taped to the arms, lower back, or neck. A stereo headphone plays back the sounds that are produced by the changes in the muscle's state of relaxation.

"Biofeedback, in effect, is like a mirror, because all the hardware does is make you aware of something that is going on all the time in your body," is what Criglar told his patients. I first met him when I was a graduate assistant in psychology, studying biofeedback as a potential tool for mapping states of consciousness.

In the late 1960s, psychologists who had been looking for some way to quantify and describe states of consciousness heard that investigators in Japan had applied EEG electrodes to the scalps of Zen monks. The Japanese investigators had found the meditation experts to emit a larger than normal amount of a certain brainwave—the relatively mundane though much discussed "alpha frequency." Shortly thereafter, investigators in India came up with similar, and even more provocative, findings when they attached their thin wires to the scalps and chests of yogic meditators. Put that together with Joe Kamiya's discovery at the University of Chicago—that people can learn to increase or decrease the amount of alpha frequency in their brainwave output—and you have the foundations of biofeedback research. Conscious control of biological functions that Western scientists had previously regarded as "autonomic" processes beyond the power of the will is a notion that carries significant implications far beyond the issue of states of consciousness.

Yogis have been claiming for a long time that people can learn to control their unconscious bodily processes and get a "permanent high," if that is one's desire. We know now that our brain, heart, and muscles generate faint electrical signals as a result of natural processes. We can observe these signals and gain valuable diagnostic information; the electrocardiagram, for example, can tell a heart specialist a great deal about the patient's health. But when the patients themselves, rather than the doctors, begin to look at those signals at the same time they are recorded, you have biofeedback. It isn't too different from yoga, except your concentration tool is not a mantra or a mandala but a microprocessor-controlled bioamplifier. It isn't instant enlightenment, any more than a book or an hour of meditation is an instant education—you still have to work for the benefits.

The perfectly legitimate but no more than promising findings about Buddhist monks and alpha frequencies were adopted as a new kind of technological gospel by some human potential faddists of the 1970s. The "alpha state" was peddled along with mood rings and expensive mantras. The popular mythology was of some kind of "electric satori"—a "plug-in" high. The fad disappeared when people realized that the alpha state is a useful and pleasant frame of mind that all people drift in and out of thousands of times every day. It can be used to help people relax, but it doesn't compare as an intoxicant to a few sips of alcohol or puffs of marijuana. The real promise of the technique is not what it does to the patient or practitioner, but what people can use it to achieve on their own initiative. Alpha isn't nearly as interesting as the ability to turn it on and off at will—like taking the wheel of your own brain.

"Biofeedback is mostly a mental exercise on the part of the patient," is the way Criglar sees it: "It's a kind of calesthenics for your consciousness. Electronic amplifiers don't do anything but help us sense those processes, bring them to our attention. Like a mirror, biofeedback shows us a part of ourselves we don't normally see. When you use what you can now sense in order to learn how to control those processes, it becomes more significant than a matter of feeling good."

The future of biofeedback devices depends on developments in two separate but related areas—fundamental research into the *meaning* of those electronic signals (the relationship between brainwave patterns and different kinds of thoughts or other mental activities, for example) is necessarily the first development. The next step is therapeutic application of that knowledge to show people how to control their own body-mind processes by making those processes visible via sophisticated display devices. Until now, fundamental research hasn't yielded much more than very rough correlations between biosignals and states of mind, but experiments have determined that biofeedback is capable of facilitating very powerful learning—people can learn to control the firing of *individual muscle fibers*, for example.

The display device in Criglar's laboratory was a tone generator. But what if his patients could learn to relax specific muscles or muscle groups by watching an animated, colored, high-resolution image on a large television screen, and listening to wraparound sound? Today's video displays, even on the most expensive computers, are only beginning to approach the degree of sophistication (scientists call it *bandwidth*) necessary to truly capture people's attention. Neither did television, when it first got started. The first, primitive prototypes of tomorrow's "mindware" are beginning to surface: Biofeedback relaxation games for home computers now include video games in which the players can win only by learning to relax. Inner Pong, anyone?

When I set out in search of a futurologist to put all these speculations in the proper perspective, all roads led to Menlo Park, California, the Houston and Canaveral of the inner-space program. Indeed, when Captain Ed Mitchell returned from the moon, his life transformed toward a new, interior mission by a mystical extravehicular experience, Menlo Park was where he set up the Institute of Noetic Sciences. Captain Ed's gallant and surprisingly effective little organization has moved north a few miles to Sausalito. But something much larger remains, down at the end of a tree-shaded lane straight out of a prewar Frank Capra film: SRI.

The sprawling research city that started out in the fifties as the Stanford Research Institute and is now known officially as "SRI International," conducts everything from heavy-duty basic research into lasers, weapons systems, and computer science to social science programs that study values and lifestyles—for a fee. SRI clients are the Fortune 100 companies and major governmental agencies, both domestic and foreign. If you need some hard-nosed agronomic forecasts, backed up with remote-sensed satellite data, for the Amazon basin, or want to lay out a five-year budget for a medium-sized nation, SRI is where you find the goods.

Although various SRI projects had dealt with research related to human consciousness and social transformation, public attention was attracted for the first time by the revelations in popular media concerning research conducted by physicists Dr. Russell Targ and Dr. Harold Puthoff into the nature of telekinesis, remote viewing (also known as "astral travel") and other psychic phenomena. One of their more provocative published findings was that many ordinary people could learn to become as adept as the so-called gifted psychics like Uri Geller, the most notorious of the psychics who studied at SRI. Their discovery certainly hints at strong connections between what people believe and what they perceive: A certain percentage of randomly selected normal subjects, when summoned to a high-security research institution and informed by certified scientists that they are about to exhibit psychic abilities, start to describe the details of top-secret outposts in the Indian Ocean, Antarctica, and other independently verifiable locations.

Despite the lurid accounts and scary extrapolations, SRI scientists continued their exploration of psychic phenomena and altered states of consciousness for years. The negative publicity made SRI personnel even more cautious than usual about speaking to outsiders, most especially journalists. But one futurist, whom I'll call "Mack," finally agreed over the telephone to sign me through SRI's security system and sit down for a talk. He ended our initial phone call with the words: "Since you are determined to write about this, you might as well find out that you're strolling through a mine field.

"We are entering an area more revolutionary than any traditional political theory," he warned when we shook hands and went through all the security-badge-signing formalities out in the reception lobby at SRI. Later, in his paper-and-floppy-disk-littered cubicle, he expanded his cautionary introduction: "In some fundamental ways, getting high is *really* what makes the world go round. We're talking about changing the nature of our beliefs about reality when we talk about 'getting high.' The funny thing about it all is that modern research is beginning to turn up connections between consciousness and reality that were first noted, in exhaustive detail, thousands of years ago."

Mack pointed out that doctrines regarding mind and matter, such as those at the core of Buddhism and Hinduism, hold that the world we experience is an illusion, created by our learned interpretations of our perceptions. We are literally hypnotized by our culture, our education, our parents and playmates and teachers, to see the world in a certain way. Enlightenment, said these *Arhats*, *Roshis*, and *Lamas*, is what happens when you see through all the illusions. The modern research that Mack referred to includes findings from psychotherapy, anthropology, and cognitive psychology that demonstrate how our beliefs, conscious and unconscious, shape our perception of reality—and how our perception of reality can be reshaped by modifying those beliefs through drugs, hypnosis, or psychotherapy techniques.

Mack likes to phrase his theories in the form of questions: "These new drugs and old techniques—why are they surfacing *now*? They have been known to a handful of Western scholars and orientalists for centuries, but they have disseminated into the wider population only recently. The keys to higher consciousness are becoming available at a crucial point in human history. In every traditional culture, there were specialists known as fools, shamans, or gurus who were supposed to get high for the benefit of their society. Now *everybody* wants to travel on inner planes, and the secrets of the ages are out in paperback editions.

"Drug abuse is one thing—essentially, that is the act of substituting one illusion for another one—but true dehypnotization of more and more people might be good for society in the long run. Right here, right now, "getting high" has negative connotations. But all these explorations of alternative states of mind is a symptom of a much deeper, possibly more positive system-wide transformation. Before a society or a civilization can change in a profound way, there has to be a profound change in the way people think about themselves. Experimentation with alternate states of consciousness might be an early symptom of such a change."

Mack was referring to a study, sponsored by the prestigious Kettering Foundation, in which he and other colleagues at SRI and elsewhere had participated, on the subject of "The Changing Images of Man." That was where he found the basis for his statement about changing the state of tomorrow when we change our state of mind. The group of researchers looked at the large-scale social transformations of civilizations around the world throughout history and noted a close connection between the cultural images of what humankind ought to be and the rise and fall of social institutions. Before any group of people can assume power or freedom, they have to see themselves as creatures who are capable of performing empowering acts. All true political revolutions are settled in people's minds before they are tested in insurrections.

Throughout history, the great external events have been linked with and triggered by changes in the way people thought, by popular notions about what people are, where we originated, what we are capable of becoming. Our images of ourselves seem to change. Institutions like slavery were abandoned, after thousands of years of acceptance, only after a large population changed their mind about its legitimacy as a human institution. Before the age of exploration and the renaissance began, the population of Europe underwent a change of consciousness from a Church-centered, other-worldly perspective centered on the afterlife to a secular, here-and-now image of life on earth.

Now we face ecological suicide and the threat of thermonuclear war. Obstacles to the continuing existence of our civilization seem to be piling up faster than solutions can be found. Our civilization certainly could use some kind of rapid, widespread change in the way we think. The systematic alteration of the state of one's consciousness is going to be one of the greatest problems and greatest promises of coming decades precisely because the technological means for expanding, distorting, and transforming our mental states will surely grow more powerful at the same time that the pressures for new ways of thinking grow heavier.

If expanded consciousness, enhanced perception, amplified intelligence, boosted creativity, even psychic talents can be induced on a large scale, as some cognitive technologists believe, what are some reasonable projections for future highs? One distinct possibility is that biofeedback and other self-regulation techniques could evolve into a mental steering device suitable for exploring deep inner space. Smoking a little empathine and hopping into your inner-space chamber might one day be an acceptable stress-reduction procedure, although it will never be as popular as driving down to the local bar to get schnockered. When today's biofeedback tones and lights evolve into full-spectrum synthesized sounds and high-resolution animated color video displays, then we'll be able to lift those mystical geometries out of our skulls and examine them in the light of day.

When we learn to steer our states of consciousness, we're bound to drift into unknown zones of human relations. When you learn to drive, you'll want somewhere to go. We are a social species: Sitting alone with your mind is fun only part of the time. Once other people are added to the experience, and once the group can share symbolic indicators of their internal states of awareness, all sorts of interpersonal hoopla will break loose. Theater pieces and real-time synthesized or animated projections could be shaped as they happen by the collective physiological reactions of the audience.

Mutual biofeedback, for example, might be a step toward the ultimate aphrodisiac. Sex is a mingling of nerve ends, and orgasms are more neural than genital. The age-old rituals of physical conjunction, the ten thousand well-known ways to rub bodies together, are the physical manifestations of mental events. When the state of your mate's nervous system can be read on a display screen, sexual experience might gain a dimension or two. If good lovers are people who try to be sensitive to their partner's desires, it follows that any way of increasing mutual awareness will expand the pleasure potential of sex. And the market for new sex devices will reward any entrepreneur-inventor who combines sufficient ingenuity with a sensual turn of mind.

Ascending from the carnal level of consciousness to the

realms of the cognitive and conceptual, memory enhancement is a future high that could blow our minds in ways we can't presently recall. Sooner or later, a version of a "memory pill" will be created, and it might turn out to be the most potent high of all time. Passing tests and remembering telephone numbers would be handy, but how would it feel to have a greatly amplified power to remember? What changes would occur in your consciousness if your memory were to be augmented? According to psychologists, altering the memory would have profound effects on other parts of the psyche, for memory serves to define the present, order reality, and anchor us in the time stream. Something will happen to the meaning of pleasure and pain when we are able to erase or recall any experience in full sensory detail.

Memory enhancement could improve the way our attentional mechanisms and senses encode experience in our brains (storage), or it could improve the way we find stored information and bring it to the surface (retrieval), or both. Think about the tens of thousands of impressions streaming into your brain-filters from your eyes and ears and kinesthetic sense as you drive an automobile on a freeway, and think about the automatic censor that blocks out from your awareness all but the most immediate and relevant impressions. What do we miss when we let the world go by this way? What if you could replay your day or your year like a film, at any speed, any time you wanted? Have you ever suddenly remembered a dream you had ten years ago? Or experienced déjà vu?

To some degree, everything we ever experience is recorded somewhere in our brains. If the degree of "reality" in experience is influenced by the amount of information a sentient being can keep track of, then the world might become a thousandfold more real to those who could store the entire stream of sensations and retrieve them selectively. Would the experience of total memory be ecstatic or hellish? What prodigies of art or invention might result? It will only be possible to answer questions like these when we move beyond the taboos and ignorance and learn how to tweak the psychomolecular controls of our own cognitive instruments.

In a sense, the will to get high is now one of the most powerful moving forces behind the thrust of human evolution. If by some prodigious leap of mind a single human being were to gain complete control over all the biochemical processes in his own body for a fraction of a second, the information blast might have as much power as a supernova.

Whether they are considered sacred or rendered taboo, awareness-expanding techniques will always be available. They will always be vulnerable to abuse. With so many volunteers for self-experimentation on the consciousness-alteration front, we can expect both breakthroughs and casualties. There will always be true explorers hidden among the daredevils, the curious, and the just plain fools who are willing to get high on a rumor. Some of them will burn their fuses and wander the street with their alcoholized or tranquillized brethren. But one of them might just stumble through the door to the next world—and come back to show us all how to get there.

Dreamworks: Spirit in the Dark

I'll never forget the night I met my extradimensional redhead. Her mind was unnaturally attuned to my innermost thoughts. Her sensual intensity was almost unreal. Pleasures I had never dared to imagine seemed to flower from her every touch, and new realms of sensory possibility opened with each caress. But when the tiny, purple, glowing orchids blossomed from her fingertips and luminous petals carpeted my epidermis, my reality alarm cried out, "Whoa, there."

It began to dawn on me that this was not an everyday encounter. After all, people in real life don't generally grow orchids from their fingertips.

Could it be a dream?

Did I even want to know?

She smiled at my primitive attempts to think logically amid all that raw sensation.

How could she know my thoughts? Who's dreaming this scene, anyway?

She laughed. Then, while looking directly at me, she lifted her hands to her temples and peeled off her entire face like a used page from a notepad. Underneath her face was . . . my editor!

"Finish that damn dream article!" she roared and hurled a ballpoint pen at me. It spun slowly, wheeling majestically along a predestined course, like a comet or an ICBM. When it hit my forehead, I woke up laughing.

It took me a second to recall precisely what I was laughing about; by then, I had already grabbed the pad and pen from my nightstand. You see, I've programmed myself to awaken briefly after each of my dream cycles in order to write down messages from my inner selves to my waking self. Reading my own dreams in the morning has become my favorite meditation before facing the new day. I get out of bed knowing that I've already accomplished something, that all my internal memoranda, inspirations, revelations, jokes, warnings, adventures, night flights, hot tips, and wild hunches will be recorded in my bedside notebook.

The messages are not always as direct and as instantly recognizable as the episode of the erotic editor. But toward the end of every day, when I take the time to transcribe my previous night's notes and heed the delicate counterpoint of symbol and metaphor, I'll take a shot at resolving a social conflict, learning a valuable lesson about myself, or, more pragmatically, developing a money-making idea. I've found that I can bolster my confidence and creativity and cultivate personal wisdom without having to resort to mind-shrinkers or mood-altering drugs. It's all there in my dreams. I'm learning how to mine the precious veins of my own subconscious treasures—without leaving the comfort of my own bed.

All I knew about dreamwork when I started dabbling in it was that Freud got pretty worked up about cylindrical symbols and dark tunnels. Then Sharon, my neighborhood trend oracle, assured me that dreamwork is "probably going to become the most popular mindwarp of the 1990s." Ever since I ignored her advice to invest in a new company called Apple Computer, I've paid close attention to her trend predictions.

"The reason dreamwork is going to break out of the New-Age ghetto is that it's the only practical form of magic that's easily available to everybody," she insisted. Coming from someone who was into the *I Ching* back when my major source of social information was *Dobie Gillis*, it was an effective pitch. "Only a few people are able to find salvation, or even a little relief, through meditation or jogging or analysis. But everybody dreams. And we dream every night. The trick is to will yourself to remember your inner dramas, then to gain conscious control of the scripts. When you control your dreams, you begin to control your life."

It was a passionate little speech. I didn't notice until the next morning how skillfully she had nudged me onto the path of my own dream expedition. The morning after our conversation, I awoke with the awareness of my last dream fresh in my memory—a relatively rare occurrence. In my dream, I was looking through a door into a classroom. I could see one unoccupied chair inside, facing the front. The teacher was standing at his desk, facing the blackboard. When he turned around, I recognized him: He was me. But I couldn't get into the room. He told me I had to talk to Sharon first. Then he tapped the blackboard and smirked.

The next day, when I told Sharon about my dream, she reached into her purse as if she had been expecting to hear exactly what I had told her. She gave me the only tools I needed to become a dream-scientist—a pad of paper and a ballpoint pen. That night, I put them next to my bed. The following morning, I discovered how potent such a simple device can be.

On my nightstand when I awoke were four pages of scrawled but readable dream scenes. I could vaguely remember forcing my way out of sleep a couple of times to scribble down some notes, but I didn't have the slightest idea what was written on those pages until I looked at them in the morning light. The first entry consisted of five words that had an inordinately powerful influence on my life: "Catch ideas in dream nets." Why did that message just *feel* so right—and *who* was sending it to me? I was hooked.

Like most people, I used to believe that I forgot my dreams as soon as I dreamed them. The evidence of that first morning made it obvious that every detail of my dreams must be stored somewhere between my ears. But I had never learned how to remember them at will. Isn't there something strange about that? We twentieth-century Americans all learn how to turn on televisions, ride elevators, and open pop-top cans, but nobody teaches us how to dream. We spend a third of our lives in another dimension. You would think more people would want to know what they do in that nightly otherworld.

The fragmentary but intriguing messages I brought back from my first dream expedition forced me to acknowledge the possibility that Sharon was right, that in our very private nightly shows, each of us is given the answers to our most vexing problems. We are shown potential pathways to our most important goals, taught how to forge the keys to our greatest powers . . yet almost all of us forget, the moment we open our eyes, the lessons we receive from these inner institutes of enlightenment.

When I mentioned this curiously universal amnesia to Sharon, she gave me a bit of advice that should, in turn, prove useful to you on your own dream quests: Dreaming is a *skill*, she told me—like tying your shoelaces or driving a car. Both those activities seemed difficult when we first learned them and then grew so familiar that they became automatic. Like any skill, dreaming can be improved through practice. Sharon assured me that eventually dream-awareness becomes automatic, and the two personae who time-share my body will then begin to help each other out, instead of living unrelated or conflicting lives.

Your other self responds surprisingly well to your intentions

You simply need to know how to attract your own inner attention. The first step toward improving your dream skills is simply to get started. Keep trying, first thing every morning, morning after morning, to recall and record the dreams of the previous night. It might not be easy at first, but the sheer novelty of peeking at your once-mysterious unconscious mind will keep you motivated long enough for the first rewards to come your way. Many people will receive a positive response on their first try, as I did. For others, it might take longer. But sooner or later, you'll get the message.

When you begin to gain your first powers to observe and control your dreams, you'll realize that even the most ordinary dream has intriguing advantages over waking consciousness. Given the proper frame of mind, who wouldn't want the key to a world where the impossible becomes possible, the imaginary is real, and the dreamer is the only one who can control the production? The range and nature of sensory experiences are limited only by the imagination and will of the dreamer. Your own private version of life as you would like to live it (even the poor can have rich dreams, the lonely can find companionship, and even the ill can dream of health) or life on other planets or even life after death can be observed as clearly as a television program—*more* clearly, because in a dream you can taste, feel, fully experience your programs.

But dreams are far more potent than internal television scenarios. They are literally the keys to changing one's way of life in the waking state. As I began to receive nightly messages about the way I was living my life, it became increasingly hard to avoid facing certain facts during the day—emotional issues, like how much I truly disliked a specific task or situation or how much I really liked a certain person. They were direct clues to the resentments and attractions that bubbled below the surface of my daytime thought.

At first, it wasn't easy to make the connection between what I had written in my dream journal and what I was experiencing in my waking life. After the exhilaration of learning that messages can come through from the other self, I was faced with the hard work of figuring out for myself just what these dream-allegories *mean*. Those connections between my dreams and my life that I did perceive were very thin, almost subliminal—a vague sense that some images and events were mere sketches of something that was hidden a little deeper. There must be some system for making sense out of all the scrambled imagery in my dream journal, I thought.

At this point, Sharon entered the scene again. This time, she carried a stack of books. Four books were particularly helpful: *Creative Dreaming* by Patricia Garfield, *Living Your Dreams* by Gayle Delaney, *Dream Power* by Ann Faraday, and *Lucid Dreaming* by Steven LaBerge. I learned the most powerful lesson a dreamworker can teach: We are all the ultimate interpreters of our own dreams; in the realms of the night, we are all our own analysts and oracles, encryptors and decoders, messengers and messages. Nobody but you can tell you what your inner self is trying to say—but skilled dreamworkers can pass along helpful tips, techniques, and tools.

The results of dreamwork often seem magical when they begin to make an impact on your life. But it is dream-*work*, not dream-magic, that summons your interior genies and commands them to perform their marvels. Communication, especially with yourself, always requires effort. Some of those who have delved into the treasure-houses of their dreams before us have left maps and clues. The books Sharon gave me, and the books that those books led me to read, helped me put the pieces together.

Tracing the arcane course of oneirology (dream study) is like trying to solve a constantly shifting crossword puzzle. Oneirology is an older art than you might think. Joseph and Daniel, two of the more prominent Old Testament dream-workers, learned their craft from practitioners of traditions that were already ancient when Biblical events occurred. The most significant clues to effective dreamwork techniques are scattered among unlikely sources, hidden away on dusty shelves, in books on mythology, theology, history, anthropology, and the occult.

Dream researchers have ascertained that all human beings dream an average of one and one half hours every night. Over the course of an average lifetime, each of us spends about four years in that other dimension. Because few people in the industrial Western culture understand its language, our entire civilization has fallen into the trap of assuming that nothing useful happens in that other world. To those diligent or talented dreamfarers who have unlocked its secrets, however, the dreamworld is a gateway to knowledge and power. The reason we forget, the moment we open our eyes, the lessons we receive from these inner institutes of enlightenment is deceptively simple: We forget our dreams because nobody taught us how to remember and because our waking consciousness depends upon a kind of selective inattention to interior senses. There are many time-tested ways for retraining the inner attention processes; the knowledge has existed for thousands of years, but it is only now beginning to emerge from obscurity.

I found that a rich tradition of dream lore had long existed in many places and in many eras—from the dreamworking tribes of Malaya and the dream lamaseries of the Himalayas, to the sleep temples of classical Greece and the dream shamans of the Iroquois. Taoist philosophers foreshadowed the findings of Gestalt psychologists, centuries in advance. Thousands of years before Freud and Jung debated their theories of dream interpretation, sophisticated dreamwork systems thrived in every quarter of the world.

A few of the ancient cultures and their dream techniques seemed particularly suitable for present-day dreamwork. I studied them, put them to the test, and received the results I am about to report here. I recommend to those who are interested in dabbling in experimental dreamwork that you adopt a similar attitude: *You* are the final authority about your own mind, so don't hesitate to adopt those tricks that work for you and to discard methods that don't. This is an experimental craft, not a prescriptive science. And be aware that your own dreamwork is bound to yield different results from mine.

Dream *incubation* is the technique of using your dreams to ask for specific messages or advice that will help you in your waking life. You can even ask for help in interpreting your dreams. In former times, the entity to whom one addressed such appeals would be a god or goddess or muse. Nowadays, many people find it easier to think of these as communications to your "hidden self" or "higher self" or "subconscious." The practice derives from, and may one day return to, the realm of medicine. Indeed, the dormant connection between modern medicine and oldtime dream-religions dates back to the first true devotees of dream incubation. The oldest known documents relating to dreamwork explicitly address the use of imagery in dream induction and interpretation. An inscription on an Egyptian papyrus in the British Museum, estimated to be thirty-five hundred to four thousand years old, says: "To obtain a vision from the god Besa, make a drawing of Besa on your left hand and, enveloping your hand in a strip of black cloth that has been consecrated to Isis, lie down to sleep without speaking a word, even in answer to a question."

The secret dream-healing knowledge of the Egyptian priesthood was transported to Greece, where it became a public and extraordinarily popular body of medical knowledge. The ancient Greeks maintained over three hundred special temples at which people slept in special dormitories in order to receive healing dreams. This mixture of medicine and metaphysics has traditionally been attributed to a historical figure—Aesculapius, the healing wanderer whose serpent-twined staff is still the symbol of the medical profession.

The temples of Aesculapius, which must have had some kind of beneficial effects to keep them in continuous use for over a thousand years, consisted of an open outer compound and a restricted inner compound. Pilgrims who sought healing dreams had to sleep in the outer compound until Aesculapius appeared to them in a dream and invited them inside the special dormitory. While awaiting their nocturnal invitation, the pilgrims studied the testimonials (carved into the walls of the compound) of former patients. When a man in a fur coat, bearing a stick with serpents on it, arrived in a dream, the pilgrim would move to the inner dream-sanctum. Inside, nonpoisonous serpents were loosed to slither among the sleepers, to inspire healing dreams (and perhaps to discourage fraternization among the dreamers).

The serpents aren't used any more, but the technique of incubation has been adopted by many contemporary dream-workers. I decided to experiment with the technique after I had been noting and analyzing my dreams for a few weeks and had some confidence in the evolving power of the process. I asked myself for a dream to help me find a way to start this article. The episode of the redheaded editor with the peel-away face was the result.

Every artist, thinker, craftsperson, or inventor knows that mysterious things can happen when you "sleep" on a subject. After trying the dream-incubation technique a few times, I knew that a force indeed existed within me, a force that could be harnessed with a little attention on my part. I began to investigate more ambitious methods for coaxing my sleep-helpers to yield their secrets. Dreamwork, I continue to discover, is a way of knowledge. Nothing has to be accepted on faith and no artificial means of psychological manipulation are required, because *you* are the laboratory, the explorer, and the final arbiter of your own reality. You even have a powerful and secret ally in this quest who is now preparing to help you begin: Just by reading these words, you are initiating contact with someone you know as well as yourself (and who knows you better than you know yourself, in many ways), someone who can introduce you to talents and powers you've only dreamed about—your inner adviser. The Iroquois dreamers called it *Ondinnonk.*

Before the Puritans and their ilk arrived and started breaking up the party, some heavyweight dreamwork was happening right here in the old New World. The Iroquois Confederacy, for example, was a democratic civilization that existed on this continent long before the Constitution was framed. Indeed, Benjamin Franklin is said to have studied the Iroquois Confederacy as a guide when he helped compose the United States Constitution.

The fragments of knowledge we still possess point to the central role of dream-guidance in the Iroquois culture. Marc Barasch, writing in *New Age Journal,* had this to say of the place of dreamwork in Iroquois society:

> Many cultures have in fact used dreams as a central rite of communion, a way of harmonizing the individual with society and the palpable, if invisible, higher forces. The six tribes of the Iroquois Federation, for example, all had formalized dream rituals. A Jesuit missionary named Rageuneau, writing in 1649, noted that they believed that "a soul makes known [its] natural desires by means of dreams, which are its language." In a striking parallel to modern psychological theory, the Iroquois also believed that if this desire, which they called "Ondinnonk," were completely thwarted, the soul would revolt against the body and make it sick.[5]

Centuries later, in Vienna, Freud rediscovered what the Iroquois knew as *Ondinnonk* when he said that the repression of the desires of the *id,* through the intervention of the *superego,* leads to neurosis. And Freud also pointed out that the sometimes hideous creations of dreams are indirect evidence of the id's activities. But Freudian theory viewed the id as a monstrous thing that gravitates toward all sorts of antisocial pleasures and must be kept in line in the interests of civilization. To the Iroquois, the source of the soul's deepest desires was not a dank den of animalistic impulses, but the font of wisdom and source of guidance. Unlike the id, its impulses are not pure aggrandizement of desires but are more benevolent, life-centered, health-giving. This inner-life force can even provide helpers if we learn how to summon them.

The vision-quest was one way to find a dream-helper: Go out to the wilderness, dig yourself a hole in the ground, and fast and pray until your helper takes pity on you and appears in a dream or vision. Iroquois warriors and healers endured great personal hardships in order to win dream-friends and to summon dream-guides. By putting the power of belief, conviction, and personal sacrifice into these dream-helpers, the Iroquois shaman created a reservoir of power he could later draw upon for help in times of crisis. Something about the idea appealed to me in the most mercenary way. I considered how useful it would be to have a dream-helper or two, maybe even an entire dream workshop of internal experts who could work on my writing every night as I slept—like the shoemaker's elves in the old story.

Not long after I heard about the Iroquois and fantasized about a dream workshop, my research turned up a little-known essay entitled "A Chapter on Dreams," written by Robert Louis Stevenson, who confessed that this is exactly how some of his most famous works were written! His technique was to induce the presleep state of hypersuggestible consciousness now known as the hypnagogic state by lying in bed with his eyes closed and his arm propped up, perpendicular to the bed. He could balance his arm and drift to the borders of sleep, but if he fell into a profound slumber, his hand would fall to the bed and awaken him. In this "twilight state," his helpers did their work. Stevenson called his helpers Brownies or Little People:

The more I think of it, the more I am moved to press upon the world my question: Who are the Little People? They are near connections of the dreamer's beyond doubt; they share in his financial worries and have an eye to the bankbook . . . they have plainly learned like him to build the scheme of a considerable story and to arrange emotion in progressive order; only I think they have more talent; and one thing is beyond doubt, they can tell him a story piece by piece, like a serial, and keep him all the while in ignorance of where they aim. Who are they then? And who is the dreamer?

Well, as regards the dreamer, I can answer that, for he is no less a person than myself . . . and for the Little People, what shall I say they are but just my Brownies, God bless them! who do one-half my work while I am fast asleep, and in all human likelihood, do the rest for me as well, when I am wide awake and fondly suppose I do it for myself. That part which is done while I am sleeping is the Brownies' part beyond contention; but that which is done when I am up and about is by no means necessarily mine, since all goes to show the Brownies have a hand in it even then. . . .

I can but give an instance or so of what part is done sleeping and what part awake, and leave the reader to share what laurels there are, at his own nod, between myself and my collaborators; and to do this I will first take a book that a number of persons have been polite enough to read, "The Strange Case of Dr. Jekyll and Mr. Hyde." I had long been trying to write a story on this subject, to find a body, a vehicle, for that strong sense of man's double being which must at times come in upon and overwhelm the mind of every thinking creature. . . . For two days I went about racking my brains for a plot of any sort; and on the second night I dreamed the scene at the window, and a scene afterward split in two, in which Hyde, pursued for some crime, took the powder and underwent the change in the presence of his pursuers. All the rest was made awake, and consciously, although I think I can trace in much of it the manner of my Brownies. . . .

It is interesting to note that one symbolic message of this dream is clear to any experienced dreamworker: Jekyll and Hyde are recognizable symbols of the dual nature of every human being, including the mass of repressed, fear-inducing knowledge that Jung called the shadow!

When I found out about the Iroquois, I realized that I had encountered a version of my *Ondinnonk*. The fact that many of these preindustrial cultures seemed to have a handle on the questions I was confronting in my own dreamwork led me to further research, which led, in turn, to more revelations. The most amazing dream culture of them all, one with practical applications to everynight dreamwork, was that of a remote Malayan tribe known as the Senoi. In the early thirties, Kilton Stewart, an anthropologist trained in psychoanalysis—sort of a Jungian Indiana Jones—introduced to the Western world the Senoi system of collective dream engineering.

The Senoi, Stewart noted in his monograph, *Dream Theory in Malaya*, are "perhaps the most democratic group reported in anthropological literature." After studying their society, which is conspicuously devoid of war, violent crime, and mental illness, Stewart concluded that "they have arrived at this high state of social and physical cooperation . . . through the system of psychology which they discovered, invented, and developed. . . ." That system of psychology, as reported by Stewart, is based upon dreamwork.

Each morning, the entire Senoi extended family unit of around thirty people would gather in the communal longhouse for a leisurely, chatty breakfast. The talk would turn to the marvelous news dispatches from the dreamworlds. Starting with the children, everyone would describe his or her dream adventures from the previous evening. The elders and other members of the group would then offer suggestions about how to interpret the dream vision, and most importantly, how to act in future dreams of the same kind.

If, for instance, a Senoi child reported a fearful dream about falling, the community would praise the child for having the courage to remember and report the experience, and an elder would explain that a falling dream is a wonderful omen, an offer of power. The child is instructed to relax and *keep falling* the next time it happens, and thus learn how to fly! When flight is achieved, the youngster is told to fly somewhere and bring back a gift to share with the tribe—a song, a poem, a design for a basket, a dance, a story, an idea. Senoi children grow up knowing that there is a proper way to act in dreams, just as Western children learn that there is a proper way to act at the dinner table; they also find out that there is much to be gained by giving themselves to the dream adventures instead of fleeing them.

One of the most progressive aspects of Senoi dream theory is their enlightened attitude toward sexual pleasure in dreams. While we in the West learn to be ashamed of erotic dreams, the Senoi learn to attain the highest possible pleasures in such dreams, and remember to ask their dream-lovers for gifts. After all, the figures who frighten you and attract you are nothing other than frightening and attractive aspects of yourself. You are frightened and attracted to these aspects for specific reasons. When you discover the true reasons for your fears and attractions, you grow. That's the gift your personal dream-lover or dream-ogre—and nobody else—can give you.

The most useful aspect of Senoi dream philosophy is the belief that you can and must *act* within your dreams, rather than experiencing them as a passive, helpless observer. If something frightening is chasing you, then you should turn around and confront it! Demand of your dream-demons that they explain themselves to you, say the Senoi, and these messengers in disguise will take off their masks and hand you their secrets. Don't run—turn around and face it! That's the only way to get the reward your bogeymen are trying to give you. According to Senoi principles, you can change the course of your dreams while you are dreaming.

I found the idea that you can act within your dreams in order to change their outcome to be a very powerful notion, for it leads to the more radical idea that *changes in your dreams can affect your waking life.* One of the longer-term effects of dreamwork is the way you tend to get acquainted with your own many personae as they pop up unpredictably in new and different guises in dream after dream—a little bit like the way soap-opera addicts get to know the characters whose fictional lives they follow for years. For those who are inclined to Jungian ideas, the *persona*, the *shadow*, the *anima* and the *archetypes* are all in there, waiting to be recognized.

Between the dreamworkers of the ancient world and the new breed of eclectic, scientifically-oriented dreamworkers of the late 1980s, were the great pioneers of Western psychology—Freud and Jung. It is hard to imagine, in the jaded late twentieth century, what a heated and venomously negative reaction greeted Sigmund Freud when he proposed that dreams represent symbolic renderings of thoughts and impulses that the dreamer had repressed because they were so primitively antisocial. Although the notion that all these potent dream symbols could be traced back to some kind of childhood sexual frustration was rejected by Freud's colleague Carl Jung and others, nobody who attempts to study dreams would dispute the fact that Freud single-handedly rescued the science of oneirology from obscurity.

Today, words like *subconscious* and *unconscious* are part of the popular vocabulary. Around the turn of the century, when Freud suggested that we all have dark closets in our minds where we keep naughty thoughts, people reacted quite violently. Today, strict Freudian theory is confined to a relatively small orthodoxy, while scores of newer theories have included collective unconsciousness, cosmic consciousness, supraconsciousness, and other parts of the vast silent regions of the mind. But Freud deserves the homage of all modern dreamworkers for his feat of recovering dream study in the West from its long slumber.

Freudian dream theory is based on the dogma that irrational and forbidden wishes and feelings are constantly generated by the *id* but are "censored" before they reach ego-consciousness.

This censorship continues even into sleep, where the dream censor preserves sleep by turning disturbing expressions of repressed material into symbolic disguises that will discharge the impulse without waking the dreamer. Furthermore, Freud asserted that important clues to the origin of neurotic symptoms could be traced back to psychosexual episodes by means of clues revealed by dreams. If the analyst and analysand can crack the dream-censor's code, together they can find the source of neuroses.

Jung, who began to think of dreams as snapshots of the human psyche, developed a hypothesis that the common dream symbols he observed cropping up in his patients' dreamwork— dark figures, wise old men, mythical beasts, beckoning young women, snakes swallowing their tails, etc.—were evidence that the human unconscious is deeper, in a sense, than the personal unconscious that Freud had mapped. Just as our species has a common biological substratum, Jung suspected that there was a common psychological substratum as well, a *collective unconscious* that includes all the tendencies and psychic potentialities inherent in human beings. In order to test his hypothesis, Jung knew he would have to travel beyond the confines of upper middle-class European society. He began to look at fairy tales, myths, the wisdom literature of India, China, and Tibet. He also began to travel to preliterate societies to observe their cultural processes firsthand.

Jung's travels in East Africa during the 1920s led him to the discovery that many of the tribes he visited and observed not only used sophisticated methods for interpreting dreams but often made the same distinction he made as a psychoanalyst between ordinary dreams that relate to the day-to-day life of the dreamer and "big dreams" that signal pivotal points in the dreamer's psychological development and prompt the dreamer to experience more profound aspects of the dreamer's humanness and gain new understanding regarding the dreamer's place in the universe. This clue led Jung to a study of recurrent themes in mythology, which led him to formulate his theory of *archetypes*, or universal symbols that emerge in art, myth, and dreams, and which can act as guides to self-transformation.

After Jung, a small but distinguished portion of the psychoanalytic community continued to develop tools for using dreamwork as a means of growth—Roberto Assigioli and Frederick Perls foremost among them. Ann Faraday and others of the Gestalt-influenced school of dreamwork helped me recognize that many of my dreams featured the same two basic characters in varied disguises: One is always meek, impulsive, sensitive, and often sneaky; the other is bold, authoritarian, censorious, and delights in catching the other fellow in the act of minor wrongdoing. The late Fritz Perls, developer of Gestalt therapy, had a handle on those two characters. He called them the Topdog and the Underdog.

One of the main principles of Gestalt therapy is that every character, setting, and situation in a dream represents distinct facets of the dreamer's personality. This is not a new idea, by the way: Buddhist psychology posits that the entire *world* is such a dreamer, that the dreamer is God, and that God is each one of us; the only difference between us is whether we have awakened to Godhood yet. Perls was an earthier guy than the Buddhist psychologists, however, and his dream-characters are earthier, as well.

The Topdog, that slightly sadistic, overly authoritarian, rigid enforcer of rules who pops up in one form or another in even the freest, least neurotic person's dreams, was viewed by Perls as an internal reflection of all the dos and don'ts laid on us by society and personal experience. Topdog is a slightly slapstick personification of the Freudian superego—an internalized nagger, prude, wet-blanket, and censor. The Underdog is generally that irrepressible, mischievous, vital part of ourselves that is usually kept under control by the Topdog, lest it cause us to lose our dignity, a situation Topdog finds acutely painful. In dreams, stern schoolteachers and prison guards are Topdogs. The passionate lover beneath the icy exterior is an Underdog, as is the thin person who is said to live inside every fat one.

In Gestalt dreamwork, the dreamworker sits in one of two chairs and verbally interviews the different parts of herself. Then she moves to the other chair, assumes the role of Topdog or Underdog, and answers her own questions. It's amazing what you will tell yourself if you simply take the time to ask. Through the dialogue of dream symbols, speaking to one another through her, she encourages her Underdog to stand up to her Topdog (shades of the Senoi!) instead of evading or sneaking around her. She persuades her Topdog to loosen the reins, assures the internal guardian that the whole system won't run amok if Underdog has a little fun. When the overcontrolling and the impulsive parts are reconciled through dream messages, the dreamworker opens her own life to richer experiences.

Once you are able to seize control of your dreams and shape them to your satisfaction, you will free yourself from the restraints of time and space. Feeling lonely on your internal itinerary? Cuddle up with Cleopatra or chat with a centaur. Feeling artsy? See the great paintings of history . . . in colors you never saw before. This isn't dull, drab, ordinary waking life, where words like *reality* and *impossible* still make sense. This is the dream state, where anything can happen. And those who have mastered the art of *lucid* dreaming (i.e., becoming aware that you are dreaming and consciously directing the course of the dream), know this very well.

Lucid dreaming is the key to the final door to dream freedom, but even the most enthusiastic dreamwork guides warn that it can't be mastered instantly, except for a talented minority of the population. Although lucid dreams are rare over the course of a lifetime, most people have moments when they come very close to the realization that they are dreaming. Flying dreams, for example, can easily launch lucid dreams, because if your dreamself is doing something as improbable as flying, chances are good that your dream ego is going to suspect that you're asleep.

Next time you find yourself flying in a dream, try testing the dream reality. If you discover that you can pass your hand through a dirigible cruising at 30,000 feet, you might "awaken to your dream," which is the first step in seizing control. As soon as your dream ego figures out that you are dreaming, you must be very careful not to wake up all the way. The next step is to maintain lucidity and rearrange reality. See if you can make the sun rise and set on command. When that works, get bolder: Fly to Paris and eat at Maxim's.

The lucid state is a getaway to many realms. In the most pragmatic level of life-enhancement, it enables you to go through "dress rehearsals" of important events. Coupled with an understanding of the messages transmitted by your nonlucid dreams, the ability to *re-create important dreams while you are lucid* raises the whole art to a new level. Instead of carrying messages back and forth between your dreamself and your waking ego, you can directly communicate with your hidden parts. If you have a problem to work out, you can try working it out consciously, in the dream.

Psychoanalysis is a process of digging for the meaning of certain psychological traumas and blockages that prevent the full healthy expression of the personality; psychoanalysts and analysands believe that by recreating these feelings on the couch, they will be able to resolve them in other parts of life. In much the same way, problems that are discovered, analyzed, and confronted in dreams might have a powerful generalizing effect on waking life. Dr. Stephen LaBerge of Stanford, the author of *Lucid Dreaming,* has conducted experiments with many dream voyagers (he calls them oneironauts), and is convinced that lucid dreams can be incubated. He is also convinced that the experience of lucidity not only bears a relationship to the self-transformation that is the goal of psychoanalysis, but also is related to the "awakening" or "liberation from illusion" that is the goal of many Eastern philosophical disciplines, such as Vedanta or Buddhism. After all, if "awakening from the dream that is life" happens to be your goal, awakening in your dreamlife might well be a good way to practice that skill. After you've attended all the orgies and feasts you want, simply instruct your dream-control center to show you your highest self.

The use of dreams in spiritual practice is firmly rooted in both Eastern and Western traditions. Every major religion in the world affords a major place to the significance of a special kind of dream; indeed, many of the scriptures of the world's great religions were received in dreams by the mortals who wrote them down. No matter which religious tradition you use to approach your spiritual path, there is a deep and significant reverence for dreamwork as a way of getting acquainted with your soul.

In the ancient Hebrew tradition, the God of Israel directly inspired his people in laws and knowledge that was transmitted through the visions and dreams of the prophets: "If anyone among you is a prophet, I will make myself known to him in a vision, I will speak to him in a dream" (Num 12:16). Joel, one of the later prophets, conveyed Jehovah's message that divinely inspired dreams would not always be reserved for prophets: "I will pour out my spirit on all mankind. Your sons and daughters shall prophesy, your old men shall dream dreams, and your young men shall see visions. Even on the slaves, men and women, will I pour out my spirit in those days" (Jl 2:28–29). The passage from Joel has particular significance to Christians as well as Jews, for the New Testament records that on the day of Pentecost that very passage from Joel was quoted in Peter's first words to the assembled crowds.

Another story in the Old Testament, that of Jacob's dream, has particular significance to the Jewish tradition, for it is both a symbolic and a direct statement of the covenant between the Children of Israel and their God:

Jacob left Beer-sheeba and set out for Haran. He came upon a certain place and stopped there for the night, since the sun had set. Taking one of the stones from that place, he put it under his head and lay down on that spot.

He had a dream: a ladder (or stairway) was set on the ground, with its top reaching to the sky; and the angels of God were going up and down on it.

And there was Yahweh standing beside him and saying:

"I Yahweh am the God of your forefather Abraham and the God of Isaac; the ground on which you are resting I will give to you and your offspring. . . ."

Jacob awoke from his sleep and said, "Truly, Yahweh abides in this site, but I was not aware!" Shaken, he exclaimed, "How awesome is this place! This is none other than the abode of God and the gateway to heaven!" (Gen 28:10–22)

Some dreamworkers have interpreted this passage to symbolize the dream's role as a mediator between the worlds of flesh and the spirit, and the ascending and descending angels are metaphors for the dreamer's transition between different levels of reality. And, by this interpretation, this passage is an explicit statement that the dream state is a gateway to the highest spiritual state. Islam, which reveres the prophets of the Old and New Testaments, includes the mystic tradition of Sufism; the Sufi mystic al'Ghazali wrote about angels as symbols of invisible forces that ascend from the source of life and the material world to the higher realms, and represent "the higher faculties in human nature."

In the New Testament, Christ's conception was announced to Joseph in a dream (Matt 1:20). And there was the case of the dream of Pilate's wife, before Pilate was to pass judgment: "his wife sent word to him; 'Have nothing to do with that righteous man, for I have suffered many things because of him today in a dream.'"

Dream-transmitted knowledge has particularly deep significance to Moslems because their holy scripture, the Koran, was received by the Prophet Mohammed in a dream. This transmission, known as the Night Journey, occurred when Mohammed, a poor camel driver, "was sleeping between the hills of Safa and Meeva, when the Angel Gabriel approached," leading El-boraq, the silver mare of miraculous powers who bore the Prophet to Jerusalem. In Jerusalem, the Prophet prayed with Abraham, Moses, and Jesus, then ascended on El-boraq through the seven celestial spheres, across oceans of white light, finally to approach Allah, the One God. All in a dream.

A Sanskrit scripture from India attests to the importance of imagery-*creation* as well as concentration on remembered images in the quest for dream-truths. The Vedic myth of Usa involves a maiden who dreamed that she made love with a man she had never met, even though she was a virgin. She told her friend Citralekha about her dream, and her friend drew pictures for her, of "all the gods, demons, human beings, and other creatures in the universe." Finally, Usa recognized the one young man in her dream, and eventually met him in waking life. The punch line of this myth is that the name *Citralekha* is translated as "Sketcher of Pictures."

The inner symbolic meaning of this reference is made clear in several related myths: The "sketcher of pictures" symbolizes the capacity of every human mind to carry meanings back and forth between different levels of consciousness in the form of imagery. It is, therefore, to every dreamworker's advantage to use tools that awaken and empower the interior "sketcher of pictures." The use of "skillful means" (*upaya*) like dreamwork was part of a step-by-step discipline for attaining self-mastery and self-realization—yoga.

Although only the dedicated few actually attain the direct experience of godhead that is the goal of yoga, the masses of ancient India were able to participate in the transformation of human consciousness, the awakening of the *inner* sense of sight that had been discovered by the authors of the Upanishads, the

Yoga Sutras, and other texts. Through myth and legend, even the uneducated were able to hear the story of the god who lost its god-consciousness in the world of illusion. Hundreds of folktales involving dreams and dreamers of "once upon a time" still convey important symbolic knowledge to the tens and hundreds of millions of people in the small villages of India. In the words of Wendy Doniger O'Flaherty, author of *Dreams, Illusions and Other Realities:*

> The Indian myths of dreaming dissolve the line between waking and dreaming reality by dissolving the distinction between a shared waking world and a lonely dreaming world, or they make it possible to drag back across the still acknowledged border between the worlds those dreams that enrich and deepen the reality of the waking world. The philosophical goal of many of these myths is to dissolve the line, but the secret agenda of many of them is to understand the reality of life through the insights that come from dreams.

The Buddhist philosophers, heirs to the Sanskrit legacies, were also interested in dreams. Indeed, the name of the Buddha literally means "the awakened one." The Indian Buddhist work on dream yoga is extensive, and it also migrated to Tibet, where Tibetan Buddhists combined Indian concepts with their own ancient shamanistic traditions to create a complex and sophisticated dreamwork technology. Judging from what their scriptures and adepts claim, the Tibetan Buddhists evolved one of the most sophisticated dream-manipulation technologies of the ancient world, East or West, complete with maps of the dream realms and specific prescriptions for exercises in dream-mastery. The nature of dreams and methods of dreamwork are closely linked in the Tibetan Buddhist worldview with the nature of reality and methods of achieving enlightenment. More properly, the Tibetans would speak of "liberation" rather than just "enlightenment," because a person's enlightening realization of the nature of reality (the "Great Awakening") leads to that person's liberation from the wheel of karma.

To discover who is dreaming the dream of your life, as a step toward waking up from all dreams, is the goal of Tibetan meditation techniques. The Tibetan-educated Western Lama, Anagarika Govinda, put it like this in his classic *Foundations of Tibetan Mysticism:*

> . . . the centre of human consciousness is empty and beyond all limiting definitions. The centre is surrounded by five sheaths which, in ever-increasing density, crystallize around the inner point of our being. The densest of these sheaths is the physical body, built up through nutrition; next is the subtle or etheric body, nourished by breath; next is the thought body or personality, formed by active thought; the fourth is the body of potential spiritual consciousness; the fifth is the body of blissful, universal consciousness, experienced only in a state of enlightenment. The development of full lucidity in waking life and dream life is an essential step towards understanding the interpenetration and relationship of these aspects of the Self.

The claims of the Tibetan dream masters and the symbolism of Sanskrit dream mythology undoubtedly serve important purposes to those on the spiritual path. Unfortunately, the spiritual value of a discipline is not necessarily a measure of its market value in this pragmatic, materialistic age. It is natural in a culture where dreamwork is neither taught nor respected for people to be skeptical of the notion that valuable information can be obtained from dreams. What the majority of the skeptical population doesn't realize is how much of what they see around them originated in a dream! The colors in your clothing, the medicine in your medicine cabinet, the synthetic materials in practically everything in your house are the results of the science of organic chemistry; the famed story of Kekulé and his dream vision of the benzene ring attests to the subconscious origins of one of the fundamental discoveries that led to the modern science of organic chemistry. And since science and technology constitute the most powerful mythologies of industrial civilization, his story links the older and newer vessels of dream knowledge.

Kekulé was one of many who tried to solve the difficult problem of describing the physical structure of the benzene molecule. Chemists knew that a group of carbon atoms formed the chemical skeleton of the molecule, but had no idea how they were arranged. Kekulé was the first to realize that they were arranged into a closed chain, a loop-like structure now known as the "benzene ring," which forms the elementary building block of those hexagonal structures that chemists draw to this day when they describe the structural properties of an organic substance. The discovery signaled a fundamental breakthrough that led to new worlds of theoretical and applied knowledge.

At the end of his career, at a banquet of the world's most distinguished chemists, given in his honor, Kekulé revealed the secret of his great discovery:

> One fine summer evening, I was returning by the last omnibus . . . through the deserted streets of the metropolis. . . . I fell into a reverie, and lo! the atoms were gambolling before my eyes. Whenever, hitherto, these diminutive beings had appeared to me, they had always been in motion; but up to that time, I had never been able to discern the nature of their motion. Now, however, I saw how, frequently, two smaller atoms united to form a pair; how a larger one embraced two smaller ones; how still larger ones kept hold of three or even four of the smaller; whilst the whole kept whirling in a giddy dance. I saw how the larger ones formed a chain. . . . I spent part of the night putting on paper at least sketches of these dream forms.[6]

This image, or quasi-hallucination, of dancing atoms in the form of "diminutive beings" continued to haunt the chemist but did not immediately lead to his famous insight. The moment of illumination, in which the image engendered a new understanding of the role of carbon atoms in many molecular structures, came years later in the form of a dream that he recounted to his fellow chemists:

> I turned my chair to the fire and dozed. Again the atoms were gambolling before my eyes. This time the smaller groups kept modestly in the background. My mental eye, rendered more acute by repeated visions of this kind, could now distinguish larger structures, of manifold conformation; long rows, sometimes more closely fitted together; all twining and twisting in snakelike motion. But look! What was that? One of the snakes had seized hold of its own tail, and the form whirled mockingly before my eyes. As if by the flash of lightning I awoke. . . . Let us learn to dream, gentlemen.[7]

Kekulé's advice is worth repeating to the artists, scientists, technologists, educators, philosophers, and everybody· else who struggles at the frontiers of knowledge: *Let us learn to dream.*

Somewhere in the back of my mind, that advice took root and germinated an idea. The idea grew into a project.

"What the world needs now is an insight amplifier." I can still see, in my mind's eye, the moment that thought struck me: I was leafing through half a dozen volumes of my dream journal, looking for the last time I had that dream of a busy carwash in the middle of the desert. I knew that I had experienced the same dream many months ago and had a strong feeling that it was connected to emotional turmoil in my home life, but I barely had time to maintain my journal and no time to index and cross-reference it. The thought of designing a system for augmenting dream recall occurred to me then, after about a year of diligent dreamwork. I had accumulated a stack of sketchbooks in which I had written my notes, made my sketches, and recorded my analyses. Somewhere on one of those several hundred pages was a clue to an important personal, spiritual, or creative problem, if only I could find it. How much other important advice went unheeded, simply because I couldn't find my way to where I had recorded it?

Over the course of the year I had systematized my dream journal by devoting an entire double-page spread to each significant dream, and continuing it over to another double-page spread if I had a lot to say or draw. I drew a rectangular box at the top of both pages and left them blank, reserving them for the date, title, and summary of the dream. On the left-hand page, I recorded and amplified the dream images and events at the top, directly under the title-box; drew a line across the bottom of the dream scenario and wrote a few words under the line about what was happening in my waking life; drew another line under the waking-life section; and left the bottom quadrant of the left-hand page blank so I could come back and attempt an interpretation after I finished working on the right-hand page of the journal.

On the right, I tried to draw a sketch or a diagram, even if it was just a stick figure, or a scribble or two that "felt right" to capture the visual feeling of the dream. The object was not to attempt to visually depict the dream scene—I'm not exactly a professional artist, and who has the time to draw out all their dreams?—but to jog my "right brain" thinking processes through the mechanism of image-creation, which seems to call into play those intuitive faculties. After I had recorded a few notes from my bedside notebook, sketched a couple of images, and tried one or another dreamwork technique, I would write a descriptive title and the date in the box on the top of the left page, then jot down a dozen-word summary of the dream in the box on the right page—as an aid to future browsing.

After these steps, I was usually ready to venture an interpretation. If not, I left the interpretation quadrant blank, for I knew from experience that the meaning of dreams a few nights or weeks ago only becomes clear when the dream-messengers change their disguise and the message finally becomes clear to my waking, journal-keeping mind. I found that the process of browsing for blank interpretation boxes sometimes jogged my pattern-recognition capabilities, and suddenly I would see the outlines of a dream message that had repeated itself in different forms. And when I had the feeling that I could find a clue to a present interpretation in a previous dream, the summary and title boxes helped me thumb my way through the journal to the page I wanted.

But even these shorthand memory aids were overwhelmed by the sheer volume of messages. When my notebook grew into a stack of notebooks, it occurred to me that a computerized database, one that could store imagery as well as words, could help me sort through my collection of dreams and find significant patterns. Humans are great at recognizing patterns when they are presented to us in intelligible form. But we are not as good as computers when it comes to sorting through masses of information to find related items that might be part of a pattern. The trick was to join human pattern-recognition ability with computer storing, sorting, and searching capabilities. I mentioned my idea during a conversation with a friend of mine whose job is to support innovative ideas for home computer software products. The conversation led to a contract, and I spent the next nine months designing a computer program that would enable me and other dreamworkers to accomplish those tasks that seemed beyond my grasp as I sat amid my dream journals. It is my belief, and my publisher's hope, that this product could signal the advent of the first true mind-amplifiers.

Just as many people find that word processors stimulate their creative abilities simply by relieving them of mechanical tasks like formatting and revising, and spreadsheet users are able to ask "what if" questions and make high-level business forecasts because their tools take care of complex but mechanical calculations, *DreamWorks* was designed to enable users to gain direct, immediate access to the most rewarding and highly motivating aspects of dreamwork, because the software takes care of the lower-level details.

Only a small fraction of the population has been able to benefit from traditional training methods. A book, after all, is a passive repository of knowledge, capable of presenting information in a static, linear form. Dreams, however, are dynamic processes in which knowledge is transmitted through graphic, symbolic, nonlinear forms. If the method of presentation could be matched with the method of thinking, computers could enable dreamwork tools to become flexible and "intelligent." So I kept in mind two fundamental psychological principles when I designed *DreamWorks:*

1. *Every person has a unique repertoire of dream symbols;* often, the meaning of these personal symbols is only revealed by examining a pattern of many dreams, unfolding over a night, a week, a month, or longer. Therefore, any system for keeping track of dreams must include an indexing and retrieval method for making these patterns visible.

2. *Images are the language of the unconscious* (or the coding mechanism for right-hemisphere cognition, if you prefer a more contemporary model). Your deep self sends messages to your waking selves in the form of pictures, visual puns, visions, and images. And you can communicate with your own deeper selves by couching our communications in the language of imagery. Computer-based graphics tools and image libraries now make it possible for everybody to create personalized images to serve as inner messengers.

Many exciting recent discoveries in the fields of perceptual psychology, cognitive science, education, and consciousness exploration have uncovered the important role of image encoding and decoding in our mental life. When I first became comfortable with the use of all my dreamwork tools, I found that I was able to use *DreamWorks* to create my own incubation images, in a computerized variant of the "Egyptian method" for awakening the mind's eye. As in many other symbolic rituals, the power of the Egyptian method is not in the name of the Egyptian gods or the precise words of the incantation, but in *the intentional focus of attention on the part of the dreamworker* required by the protocols of the ritual. Computer graphics can concentrate one's focus of attention and thus amplify the power of the age-old ritual.

Although in the current era most people don't consider themselves to be artistically gifted, in many other times and places the act of sketching, sculpting, or painting the visions seen in dreams has been considered to be a natural part of most people's social repertoire. So I built into *DreamWorks* a means of empowering and awakening anyone's internal image-artist, whether or not they consider themselves "artistic" or a "visual thinker," through the capabilities of the *Image Bank*. By choosing from a selection of built-in images—modifying, mixing, matching, and creating new ones using graphic editing tools—I found that I was able to grow fluent in a graphic vocabulary in a short period of time. Now, when I open my electronic dream journal, it takes a matter of minutes to record my dream, designate key words and images for my dream database, and create a page of visual analogies and images to go along with the text. When I want to find out which other dreams contain flaming giraffes, or occurred on Friday nights, I simply query my dream database and the key dreams pop up on my "dreamscape."

The keys to unimaginable power are within the reach of the entire terrestrial population. I am certain that the next leap for our species will not be launched from the factories of physical technology, but from the night flights of creative dreamers. Think about the possibilities: A visit to an island paradise where intelligent natives sing solutions to your everyday problems, a family conference that includes your departed grandparents and your unborn children. In one night, you could philosophize with Aristotle, joke with W. C. Fields, talk investments with J. P. Morgan, and work out with the Olympic gymnastic champion. Can you still call it "only a dream" or "a figment of the imagination" when the solutions invented by your dream consciousness work in your daytime life?

Even if it is only remotely possible, the potential rewards of controlling our dreams seems well worth pursuing. Sensual pleasure, practical knowledge, creative inspiration, inner wisdom, emotional tranquillity, extrasensory perception, or even a hot tip for the seventh race at Belmont—whatever the quest, the answer may be awaiting for you just beyond the borders of sleep.

Vizthink

Our eyeballs are assaulted with more raw visual information in a typical day than our great-grandparents assimilated in a year. I call it *vizblast*: future shock of the optic nerve.

We are bombarded by images from the moment we open our eyes in the morning until we close them at night. When we sleep, the images assume different shapes and we call them dreams. At this moment, billions of earthlings around the globe are confronted by trillions of photos, videos, films, symbols, pixels, signs, logos, and pictographs on billboards, magazines, newspapers, movie screens, television sets, graffiti, and computer terminals. Most of the images seem to flow through our nervous systems unhindered by conscious awareness, like so many neutrinos zipping silently through the planet.

Maybe vizblast is harmless. Probably not. Unless we can find something constructive to do about it.

Despite the incessant storm of visual symbols, few of us in this high-viz culture consider ourselves capable of expressing ourselves visually, or of using images to communicate. We go to professionals for that. In light of the evidence that binocular eyesight has been a mainstay of our species' bag of survival traits for millions of years, isn't it strange that visual communication is not a common language outside advertising agencies and art schools? Eyeballs, after all, are where brains meet the world. Which means that something unprecedented must be happening to our *minds* as a result of this recent upturn in optic input.

Very few people ever call it by name, but we are a visually illiterate culture. Everybody knows how to talk, most people know how to write a sentence, everybody seems to believe they could write a book, but most people believe that only artists and illustrators are capable of communicating visually. Blind spots like this are usually worth examining, because they sometimes indicate a way of apprehending the world that *requires capabilities of our perceptual apparatus that we haven't learned to use yet*. If you can't read, you don't pay too much attention to all the text in your environment, but this deficiency is easily cured by education. The same can be said for visual thinking.

New communication technologies and new knowledge about how the human mind functions are changing the traditional attitude that visual expression is reserved only for the "talented." And the pace of change seems to be quickening because of the continuing development of graphics-based personal computers. The psychological and technological tools for augmenting human intellect we have today are but the earliest generations in a rapidly evolving technology; judging from the computer systems now on the drawing boards, the tools themselves soon will *show* people how to use them.

Most importantly, *the new revolution is not just about new tools. It's about a whole new way of using tools.* Like all revolutions, it's about a new way of seeing.

Those old prejudices about talent and visual expression have been jogged out of their tracks by several recent discoveries. One eye-opener was the discovery that visual thinking influences our reasoning processes: Experiments by perceptual psychologists revealed that our perceptions, particularly our visual perceptions, structure the way we think about the world. Another area of discovery emerged from the design of new ways for people to use computers, a field in which the development of a graphic vocabulary plays a key role. At the creative end of the consciousness spectrum, the use of imagery for communicating abstractions the way artists and designers do seems to involve a specific set of mental skills. Western educators in kindergartens and graduate schools are beginning to develop methods for training these skills.

Anthropologists, scholars of Eastern religions, depth psychologists, and spiritual seekers have brought to the West over the past few decades an extensive body of knowledge concerning psychological methods for evolving higher powers of inner seeing. The yogic and meditation techniques of Tibet and India include instructions and exercises for elevating the consciousness of the practitioner by concentrating on visual symbols—*mantras* or *mandalas*. The Sufi mystics of Islam and Cabalists of Judaism have described the use of detailed visualizations to achieve high forms of spiritual insight. Shamanic healers in North and South America employ sand-paintings, yarn-weavings, and other maps of the inner world. Staring at mind-maps to induce trances or other altered states of consciousness seems to be a ubiquitous human trait.

The psychologist Carl Jung gathered examples of these visualization tools from around the world as evidence for his theory that these forms emerge spontaneously from human minds in every culture and epoch because they reflect innate symbols of the nature of the human psyche, which he called archetypes. Jung also concluded that in some cases the appearance of archetypal patterns in dreams or artistic imagery herald a transformation of consciousness. Throughout the life cycle, the psyche of every individual is challenged by opportunities to shed aspects of his or her old way of seeing the world in order to adopt a wider perspective—in other words, *growth*. But growth can be painful when the psyche is faced with profound transformation. The archetypal patterns emerge from the unconscious into awareness, according to Jung's theory, as messages from the collective unconscious of the human race. These visions of wheels and crosses and spirals, shadowed figures and haloed faces, are spontaneous, universal symbols that help the individual endure the rigors of psychological and spiritual transformation. Archetypes help people envision their future higher selves, and thus pave the way for change.

Whether people want to transform their consciousness beyond the range of experiences sanctioned by their native culture's rites of passage depends on whether they believe that they have high potentials they haven't learned to use, on whether they have sufficient motivation to grow, and on whether this kind of transformation is socially sanctioned. "Normal consciousness" is largely a matter of fashion. It's consciously and unconsciously molded by cultural myths and propaganda. The degree of consciousness a person experiences in a particular time and place is determined to a great degree by the unconscious beliefs of that person's culture and era about what is proper and desirable to experience. Which leads to a possible explanation for why Western culture is visually illiterate: Visual thinking, along with intuition, has been unconsciously out of fashion in the educated world ever since the industrial revolution.

Indeed, if you weren't an artist or writer, too much visual imagination has been culturally taboo until recently. "Seeing things" used to mean that you were a candidate for a straightjacket, but nowadays it could mean you are a type A personality who is working on decreasing his hypertension through visualization or an executive preparing for a business presentation by practicing a guided imagery exercise. The taboo against inner seeing is breaking down. Suddenly, it is permissible, perhaps even fashionable, for nonspecialists to train their perceptions as well as their intellect. When the early adopters pass the word along to the mainstream population, it might finally become *acceptable,* and then vizthink will take off.

TRAINING THE MIND'S EYE

Visualization and guided imagery techniques show promise as practical tools and the use of visualization has become a topic of serious research in medicine, education, sports medicine, and organizational development. Relaxation therapies for preventing hypertension have employed guided imagery with such success that the new medical discipline of psychoneuroimmunology has emerged to study these effects. Olympic athletes, educators, and business executives are using visualization-assisted autosuggestion techniques to achieve pragmatic goals. The question no longer seems to be *whether* visualization training works, but *how* it works.

A few people have begun to suggest that just about anybody can learn visual thinking skills, just as we learn to type or write a letter. The exponents of visual education say it's mostly a matter of practicing the proper exercises and having appropriate tools. Vizthink appears to be a general-purpose tool—it can be applied successfully in many different task domains. Like the ability to read and write, the ability to think and communicate visually can be used to achieve a variety of different goals. The one aspect that connects such wildly disparate endeavors as medical self-care, psychological and spiritual growth, peak athletic performance, artistic and scientific creativity is *the power of images to program and reprogram one's unconscious belief systems.*

We call it autosuggestion. Sanskrit and Tibetan have dozens of different words for the process of reprogramming unconscious beliefs. Although every discipline adds its own trappings, most visualization exercises begin with deep physical relaxation routines accompanied by attention to the rhythm of the breath. This preliminary relaxation state seems to be a prerequisite to successful autosuggestion; it is as if the unconscious mind is more receptive to communication, particularly in the form of images, when the censoring conscious mind is lulled into a half-sleep. When deep relaxation is attained, the practitioner attempts to recall in his or her mind's eye positive memories of scenes from the past, or create images of positive scenes that haven't happened yet. A runner might visualize a cheetah, while a person with a stress-related disease might visualize a quiet meadow.

The practitioner can be a passive observer of mental images or an active shaper of them. The core procedure in all cases is the same—imagery and relaxation are paired with positive affirmation. The relaxation phase neutralizes the censoring consciousness that guards the gates of awareness. The affirmation provides the content of the reprogramming. The image affixes it into subconscious memory for later recall. The hypertensive sees an inner image of relaxation at a moment of stress, and begins to relax. During a race, the runner remembers the cheetah's fluidity, and unlocks new reserves of power.

One form of imagery discipline that has the potential for improving a lot of people's lives in the information age is the ancient practice of using mental imagery as an aid to memorization. The image-memory connection that promises to become so important in the next computer revolution was established during the Roman Empire. For more than a thousand years, before the printing press put them out of business, the intellectual elite of the Western world practiced a form of visualization exercise known as "the art of memory" or "the memory palace." The use of visualizations enabled practitioners to memorize long passages of poetry or theology by associating parts of the text with images.

Legend has it that a Roman poet was invited by a wealthy patrician to compose spontaneous verse in honor of the patron at a banquet the patrician planned to host at his palace. The poet, however, felt inspired by the occasion to compose poems to the glory of his personal gods—the twin deities, Castor and Pollux. The patron told the poet that he could collect his fees from the gods, if he liked them so much. At that moment, a servant arrived in the banquet hall, summoning the poet to the door, where two men were waiting to see him. When the poet stepped outside, there were no men waiting. But before he could step back into the palace, an earthquake struck. The marble structure toppled, crushing the host, his servants, and all the guests. Only the poet survived. The falling rubble reduced all the guests at the dinner table to an equally unrecognizable consistency, so the poet, who was the only survivor, was asked to help the families of the deceased guests identify their bodies. Because he could close his eyes and see a remembered image of the guests as they were seated at the table, the poet was able to tell the families where to find their relatives' remains. The memory palace evolved from this method.

The basic technique is to memorize the details of a room or building as one would see it on a guided tour around the premises. Once the architectural details visible along this mental tour are committed to memory, practitioners of this art associate blocks of text with certain pillars, arches, doorways, walls, furnishings, places at a banquet table—each object and attached text occupying a specific location along their guided mental tour. (In addition to the association of text with images, this technique also makes use of the memory-extending technique now known as chunking—breaking up the material into digestible chunks.) In order to "play back" the material that was memorized, the practitioner reenters the memory palace and takes the tour through the scene previously constructed in his or her mind's eye, "reading" the chunks of text that were "placed" at strategic spots along the tour.

Visual exercises can augment other mental capacities besides the capacity to memorize information. Although memorization is an important component of thinking, it is most closely connected to thinking about ideas that already exist. What about creativity—the creation of ideas that never existed before? A potentially powerful use of visualization capabilities would be the application of mental imagery techniques to the production of new ideas—inspiration in the arts and invention in the sciences. This is precisely an area of human higher functioning that seems to be the most difficult for machines to imitate, and there is considerable testimonial evidence from the best minds of the centuries that certain individuals have harnessed the creative power of mental imagery.

The role of visual thinking in artistic and scientific creativity through the ages can be discerned in a distinct pattern of historical testimony. Autobiographical accounts of creative geniuses from Mozart to Einstein attest to the role of mental images in the creation of masterpieces. Einstein remarked to his biographers that his thoughts and discoveries were closely connected to specific images that he pondered or which flashed into his mind in a moment of insight. As a young man, Einstein was fascinated by the thought of riding on a light beam and wondered what would happen if he looked at himself in a mirror while hitching one of these rides. If he rode the lightbeam backward, the light from the mirror wouldn't be able to travel faster than light, and would therefore never travel from the mirror to his eye. Years of meditation on that paradoxical image resulted in the theory of relativity, which Einstein explained to others in terms of more imagery: His *Gedankenexperiments* involving people holding yardsticks while they traveled at the speed of light, were as much "thought pictures" as they were "thought experiments" (the traditional translation of *Gedankenexperiment*).

Einstein was a vizthink novice, however, in comparison with one of his contemporaries, Nikola Tesla. Although his name isn't a household word today like Einstein's, Tesla's discoveries in the area of electrical power generation and transmission were fundamental contributions to the electrification of the world. In his autobiographical writings, Tesla revealed the way in which he used his remarkable powers of visualization to test new inventions in his mind long before he built laboratory models.

Tesla's unusual ability to imagine detailed scenes in his imagination started as an affliction rather than a valuable talent. When he was a schoolboy, he attended the funeral of a young schoolmate. The scene made such a deep and unhappy impression on the young man that Tesla found himself sitting in a classroom or walking down the street when the memory of that scene would enter his mind with such vividness it seemed as if he were witnessing it all over again. From time to time, memories of unpleasant scenes he had witnessed in the past would enter the boy's mind involuntarily. In order to free himself from these maddening apparitions, young Tesla set himself the task of gaining control of these episodes. Whenever an unpleasant image forced itself into his awareness, Tesla deliberately summoned a more pleasant image from his memory. To his relief, the technique worked.

There was only one hitch. Young Tesla discovered that pleasant memories would lose their power to counteract unpleasant images, and after using a particular image once or twice, he had to find a new one. Eventually, Tesla ran out of images of pleasant memories to summon as a talisman against disturbing imagery. So he began to travel to new, totally imaginary landscapes whenever an attack of waking nightmares threatened. He imagined himself in places he had never actually seen before. He found that the more detailed and imaginative he made his visualized journeys, the more effective they became as guardians against the terrifying sights. Tesla continued to refine this capability until he was about seventeen, when he began to think seriously of embarking on a career as an inventor.

When Tesla turned to the task of designing new machines, he was delighted to discover that he was able to visualize possible inventions with great facility. He didn't need to make models or drawings or perform experiments. He found that he was able to construct, modify, and even operate complicated mechanical devices purely by visualizing them. By the time he actually built a model, he had already tested it, fixed bugs, and added improvements simply by mentally manipulating images of the machines.

Tesla might have never achieved such momentous results if he had not been challenged by a teacher who mocked his ideas. When Tesla was a student in Yugoslavia, a dynamo of the sort then available was imported and demonstrated for his class. The young inventor, who had by that time gained a high degree of mastery over his visualization powers and considered himself well-versed in the principles of electrical engineering, pointed out that a more efficient dynamo might be built on slightly different principles. His professor lectured the class on the impossibility of what young Tesla had proposed. Humiliated and furious, Tesla took up the challenge. As he wrote, years later:

> I started by first picturing in my mind a direct current machine, running and following the changing flow of the currents in the armature. Then I would imagine an alternator and investigate the processes taking place in a similar manner. Next, I would visualize systems comprising motors and generators and operate them in various ways. The images I saw were to me perfectly real and tangible. All my remaining term . . . was passed in intense but fruitless efforts of this kind, and I almost came to the conclusion that the problem was unsolvable. . . .[8]

Although he was hoping for and working toward a breakthrough, the solution came unexpectedly to the young inventor when he and a friend were walking through a park, reciting poetry. Tesla noted later that the poem he was reciting just before the illumination occurred was Goethe's *Faust*. As the sun was setting, he was reminded of the passage:

> The glow retreats, done is the day of toil
> It yonder hastes, new fields of life exploring;
> Ah that no wing can lift me from the soil,
> Upon its track to follow, follow soaring . . .

A glorious dream! though now the glories fade.
Alas! the wings that lift the mind no aid
Of wings to lift the body can bequeath me.

Of the moment when his mental image emerged suddenly into clarity, Tesla later wrote:

> *As I uttered these inspiring words the idea came like a flash of lightning and in an instant the truth was revealed.* I drew with a stick on the sand the diagrams shown six years later in my address before the American Institute of Electrical Engineers, and my companion understood them perfectly. The images I saw were wonderfully sharp and clear and had the solidity of metal and stone. . . . I cannot begin to describe my emotions. Pygmalion seeing his statue come to life could not have been more deeply moved. . . . For a while I gave myself up entirely to the intense enjoyment of picturing machines and devising new forms. It was a mental state of happiness about as complete as I have ever known in life. Ideas came in an uninterrupted stream and the only difficulty I had was to hold them fast. The pieces of apparatus I conceived were to me absolutely real and tangible in every detail, even to the minutest marks and signs of wear. I delighted in imagining the motors constantly running, for in this way they presented to the mind's eye a more fascinating sight. . . .[9]

Tesla believed that his ability to perform complex mental modeling exercises could be taught to others and proposed that a future science of "teleautomatics" would combine visualization skills with conventional scientific thinking tools such as logic and mathematics to provide a kind of learnable mind amplification for engineers and scientists. But the idea of visual thinking as a legitimate area for study and as a possible means of enhancing the thinking process wasn't revived until the late 1960s. The first reports of experiments on "split-brain" patients came out in 1968, and Rudolf Arnheim, Professor of Psychology of Art at Harvard, published his book *Visual Thinking* in

1969. In effect, the halls of academe and the laboratories of modern science—twin pillars of modern cultural belief systems—both granted legitimacy to the idea of visual thinking as a subject worth learning.

Arnheim gathered an impressive array of evidence from ancient philosophers, laboratory experiments, educational observations, scientific writings, and the history of art to support a bold thesis. He proposed that *all* thinking, not just the kind we recognize as visual thinking, is perceptual in nature. Arnheim pointed out deep similarities between the way we see on a physiological level and the way we reason on the cognitive level. One direct consequence of Arnheim's proposed new paradigm is that the old dichotomy between the senses and the mind—seeing and thinking—is seen to be false. And if the split between perception and cognition that is built into our model of how our own minds work is illusory, as Arnheim claims, then we are failing to educate future generations in a proper manner. By ignoring perceptual training as a general thinking tool, our educational system fails to address the most pressing educational challenge of the coming decades: how to produce enough people capable of understanding and operating the complex technological infrastructure that now supports our civilization.

The split noted by Arnheim between what tradition regarded as the perceiving and reasoning parts of the human mind was complemented by contemporaneous discoveries in the field of neurophysiology. A year before *Visual Thinking* was published, Roger Sperry published his papers about the complementary functions of the two hemispheres of the human brain, and won the Nobel Prize for this work. Observations of patients who underwent surgical procedures separating the two halves of their cortex demonstrated that certain general modes of thinking seem to be specialized in one half or the other. The left cortical hemisphere appears to be more heavily involved in the modes of mental activity that proceed in a linear and logical manner and uses verbal language, while the right hemisphere usually participates in nonlinear, intuitive thinking and uses the language of images.

The phrase "right-brain thinking" entered the popular vocabulary by the 1980s, as a result of the "left-brain/right-brain" hoopla that burst out of scientific circles into pop paradigm-hood in the 1970s. The dichotomy between those functions that were concentrated in one hemisphere or the other was adopted as a New Age metaphor for everything from education to golf. Subsequent research has confirmed and extended Sperry's original findings regarding hemispheric differences but has also revealed the limitations on applying this model to human behavior. Despite the excesses of over-metaphorizing, the discoveries about interhemispheric differences do offer a framework for understanding the false dichotomy that Arnheim was pinpointing in *Visual Thinking:*

> The arts are neglected because they are based on perception, and perception is disdained because it is not assumed to involve thought.
>
> In fact, educators and administrators cannot justify giving the arts an important position in the curriculum unless they understand that the arts are the most powerful means of strengthening the perceptual component without which productive thinking is impossible in every field of academic study.
>
> What is most needed is not more aesthetics or more esoteric manuals of art education but a convincing case made for visual thinking quite in general. Once we understand in theory, we might try to heal in practice the unwholesome split which cripples the training of reasoning power.

In an era when art education is almost universally regarded as one of those frills that can be axed early in a budget crunch, it seems unlikely that local school districts are likely to turn into hotbeds of vizthink innovation. But a growing grassroots trend toward self-education might make an end run around the educational establishment. Three converging paths of social and technological change make up this trend: First, an effort on the part of a few pioneering educators to develop curricula for visual thinking skills has resulted in the creation of tools for other educators to use; the growing popularity of books about visualization or visual thinking exercises demonstrates the growing interest among the general population; and the emergence of personal computer software as a medium for visual self-education signals the arrival of a powerful enabling technology.

The arrival of highly graphical computers on desktops in the 1990s might boost the movement from the present small cadres of researchers and educators to a population-wide phenomenon. However, there is evidence that training could be more important than technology when it comes to the basics of vizthink education. With a book of exercises, some blank paper, and a pencil, it is now possible for individuals to put together a curriculum for training visual thinking skills. A few educators from the kindergartens to the graduate schools did heed Arnheim's call, and their efforts over the past decade have produced a rich selection of texts for training visual skills.

In 1975, Kimon Nicolades's book *The Natural Way to Draw* provided the first accessible primer to an aspect of vizthink training and one of the best examples of how a book can help teach a cognitive skill. Probably the most accessible, effective, and popular vehicles for do-it-yourself vizthink came along a few years later, in the form of two books by Betty Edwards. *Drawing on the Right Side of the Brain,* based on the author's experience as a teacher, showed that people who normally considered themselves to be "untalented" could be coached into an ability to draw that would be considered highly talented by most people. The entire idea of "talent," Edwards believes, is a manifestation of the same kind of illusory split that Arnheim was talking about. One of the pedagogical tricks that Edwards used in that book was a simple method for understanding the importance of shifting one's entire perspective from one way of seeing to another: She asked her students and readers to draw objects *upside down.* The book sold hundreds of thousands of copies throughout the 1980s.

Another breakthrough book about visual self-education, *Thinking with a Pencil,* by Henning Nelms, came out in 1981. Nelms articulated the key discovery that drawing is more than a part of the world of art and design. It is a thinking tool in its own right. As Nelms put it: "Practical drawings are mental tools. Once you have learned to make them, you will find that they are as useful in solving problems as saws and hammers are useful in carpentry." Another book that sold phenomenally well in the 1980s, Shakti Gawain's *Creative Visualization,* appealed to the portion of the population that market researchers call in-ner-directed. Gawain spread the idea that visualization was not just for artists, but could be used to achieve practical or spiritual goals in life.

In 1986, Betty Edwards published *Drawing on the Artist Within, a Guide to Innovation, Invention, Imagination, and Creativity.* Drawing on the emerging scientific knowledge about brain functions, autobiographical accounts of creative individuals, and the experiences of her students and the readers of her first book, Edwards accomplished on the popular level what Arnheim had proposed more formally. She demonstrated a methodology for learning how to think visually. In the introduction to her book, Edwards explains:

Yet verbal language and analytic thought have dominated human life for so long a time now that it is hard to imagine that there might be other means of translating experience, valuable for thinking yet altogether different. We have grown used to the idea of other languages, to be sure: the languages of music, of dance, of mathematics and science, the relatively new computer languages, and of course the language of art itself—certainly not a new idea. But the notion that we might benefit from a visual, perceptual language as a parallel to verbal analytic thought processes is, perhaps, an idea of our own time. . . .

Thus, everywhere I looked I seemed to find confirmation of my belief that direct perception, a different kind of "seeing" is an integral part of the thinking—and hence the creative—process. And if that was, indeed, true, I thought it would be helpful to have a means to access that vision, not in words but in a form appropriate to vision. Therefore, in searching for a key to creativity, I also began to explore ways in which to express the visual, perceptual mode of human brain function. Not surprisingly, I found such a language already in use—the language of drawing, which can record what we see, either in reality or in our mind's eye, in a way not totally dissimilar to the way we record our thoughts and ideas in words. Drawings, like words, have meaning—often beyond the power of words to express, but nonetheless invaluable in making the chaos of our sensory impressions comprehensible.

Edwards elaborates on the same key theme that Nelms proposed in *Thinking with a Pencil*—that drawing is not only a way for artists or designers to represent ideas, but can be an adjunct to thought itself, a way to gain access to new ways of seeing. Edwards stresses another point that investigators of creativity have known for some time, that productive thinking, creative problem solving, inspired art or invention, is not strictly a matter of finding and strengthening a set of specific mental skills, but of cultivating an overall facility for shifting mental gears between different ways of thinking.

Edwards's way of teaching creativity was to teach drawing. In her second book, she took her method a step further by using drawing exercises as a means of exercising that elusive ability to switch between different modes of thought—a skill that should be useful for any kind of thinking. Edwards called the mental state associated with this skill *controlled mental shifts*. She claims that drawing is not only a representational tool, but a way of controlling mental shifts, whether you are thinking about art, science, or business. Speaking of the necessity of finding a way to train people in perceptual flexibility, she notes, in the first chapter:

At present, our culture provides few opportunities for such training. We are used to thinking by means of the language system of the brain, and that mode has proved its effectiveness over the centuries. But we are only now beginning to understand the complex dual functions, verbal *and* visual, of the human brain, and new possibilities are opening up. As I see it, unlocking the doors to perception and releasing the potential for creativity is a twofold process: first, removal of the deterrent concept of talent as a requirement for learning basic perceptual skills; second, teaching and learning based on new knowledge of how the human brain works.

My claim is quite modest; if you can catch a baseball, thread a needle, or hold a pencil and write your name, you can learn to draw skillfully, artistically, and creatively. Through learning to draw perceived objects or persons, you can learn new ways of seeing that guide strategies in creative thinking and problem solving just as, through learning to read, you acquire verbal knowledge and learn the strategies of logical analytical thought. Using the two modes together, you can learn to think more productively, whatever your creative goals may be. The products of your creative responses to the world will be uniquely your own, your mark on the world. And you will have taken a giant step toward attaining a modern brain. For in the years ahead, I believe that perceptual skills combined with verbal skills will be viewed as the basic necessities for creative human thought.

With the accumulation and popularization of scientific and pedagogical knowledge about visual thinking skills, the first courses for teaching visual thinking have appeared in colleges. Stanford was the first place I spotted an accredited (and wildly popular) course. The student appellation for the course name was the inspiration for my use of the term *vizthink*.

My own encounters with the vizthink revolution came from the computer side, rather than the education side of the trend. In the mid-1980s, a technical writing assignment brought me to one of Xerox Corporation's research facilities, where I became acquainted with a wonderful conversationalist by the name of

Bill Verplank. Bill's job at Xerox at that time was to apply the principles of graphic design to the design of human-computer interfaces. (A human interface is the way the human user gives commands to the computer and receives information from the computer. The way a computer screen looks is a vital element in interface design.) Bill Verplank is not only a visual thinker but a visual communicator, which means that your eyes are usually traveling back and forth between his face and his writing surface while you converse with him; you can walk away from your meeting with Verplank clutching a handful of papers covered with hieroglyphic artifacts of the conversation. One of the first things he showed me was the way graphic design principles have become essential to the creation of computer-based tools.

Verplank was one of the founding members of the teaching team at Stanford that pioneered the course in visual thinking for undergraduates. It grew out of the school of engineering, not the art department. One of the other Stanford teachers, Robert McKim, has written *Experiences in Visual Thinking*, a book of exercises for learning visual thinking strategies and techniques. Stacks of the book can be found in the Stanford bookstore, under a big sign that says VIZ-THINK. I thought it was a new category or genre rather than just a text for a popular course when I first saw the sign. As more knowledge is contributed from the fields of psychology, education, and design, the visual thinking curriculum at the college level could blossom into a discipline in its own right—a fundamental part of the well-educated person's intellectual tool kit.

If you were to ask Mona Brookes about college courses in visual thinking, she would undoubtedly tell you that it is a good idea, but those students might have started twelve years ago, back in kindergarten, or earlier, in nursery school. Brookes, an art education specialist, teaches educators and children how to revamp their own opinion of their artistic talent in a short session. Drawing on the same knowledge about brain functions that Edwards used in her books, but applying an approach specifically tailored to the needs of students as young as four years old, in 1986 Brookes published *Drawing with Children: A Creative Teaching and Learning Method That Works for Adults, Too.* The "before and after" drawings in the book show how children can create compositions of astonishing sophistication after as little as an hour of exercises. My mother, a lifelong art teacher (now a children's docent at San Francisco's Museum of Modern Art: Hi Mom!) introduced me to this book. She's been reading it and playing with my three-year-old daughter Mamie, and they are both having a high old time. I believe these drawing curricula work well with young people because the lessons are based on what we normally consider to be "play," and young children have not yet learned that "work" is supposed to be a more acceptable way to spend their time.

As social and technological forces increase the value of visual thinking, the law of supply and demand will come into play, and means of improving visual thinking skills will become available to those who want to take advantage of them for the price of a book or a course. The question is no longer whether vizthink skills can be trained or even so much how to do it. The coming challenge will be to find ways to disseminate knowledge quickly, on a large scale. The next significant changes to take place will affect the educational delivery media.

The most dramatic changes in the way people think in their daily work and play in the 1990s will come about as the result of computers like the ones Bill Verplank helped design at Xerox, and future generations of technology that teams of designers are devising now at Apple and IBM and Japan, Inc. Computer manufacturers are paying very careful attention to visual thinking. The old dream of developing a visual thinking language is beginning to manifest itself among a small group of early adapters—on millions of personal computer screens.

*   *   *

COMPUTERS + GRAPHIC LANGUAGE = MIND AMPLIFIERS

In the past, vizthink was driven by social trends. In the future, it will be driven by technology. In the 1950s and 1960s, when computer designers built computers that were meant to be used by computer experts, they didn't devote much thought to the niceties of human-computer communications. But when the computers they designed grew powerful enough and inexpensive enough to be used by nonexperts, by the early 1970s, it became necessary to create a new way of using computers. By combining a graphic display, a pointing device, and a "point and click" syntax for selecting commands from visible menus, the designers of the new human-computer interfaces made it possible for humans to bring our highly evolved visual sense to the task of harnessing the power of the computer.

The growing use of "direct manipulation interfaces" in which computer users command computing power by manipulating elements of a graphic display means that a visual thinking syntax is being built into the next generation of computer technology. Xerox Corporation, who developed the first prototypes of these new computers, went to the trouble of hiring Bill Verplank, a professor of design, because their research demonstrated that the visual elements of a computer display can be used to augment the power of the computer-user's thinking. And their research was based on work that had been done at the dawn of the computer age by people who had visions, literal pictures in their minds, of how computers ought to operate.

The highly graphic, interactive personal computers of the mid-1990s will be new to most people, but they will be the result of a quest that spanned over forty years. The first personal computers (a desktop computer dedicated to the use of one person, rather than a large computer shared by a group) were the result of the stubborn efforts of a small group of people who saw computation as something even more important than scientific number-crunching or business data processing. In the 1960s, the personal-computer pioneers dreamed of evolving specific kinds of mind-amplifiers. In the late 1980s, we are only beginning to see the first devices that fit the specifications of those early dreams.

The quest for machines capable of augmenting human thinking dates back to "As We May Think," an article by Vannevar Bush, published in *The Atlantic Monthly* in the closing months of World War II. Bush had been President Roosevelt's science adviser and director of the Office of Research and Development during the war. As he was completing the coordination of over six thousand scientists in the war effort, the largest scientific undertaking in history, he recognized that their success was making it necessary to find new ways of keeping track of knowledge.

"The summation of human experience is being expanded at a prodigious rate, and the means we use for threading through the consequent maze to the momentarily important item is the same as was used in the days of square-rigged ships," Bush wrote. He called for the development of a device to improve the quality of human thinking—the *memex*, he called it. But nobody, not even Bush, suspected that the newborn technology of electronic computing would have any applications to individuals.

The idea that graphic computers could be used to augment human intellect was invented by Doug Engelbart, in the winter of 1950, as he was driving to work. He had been trying to think of the best way to use his education in electrical engineering to help solve humankind's problems. Most of the problems the young engineer saw facing the world were characterized by unusual urgency and complexity, so he started to think of technologies for dealing with complex, urgent problems. As he thought about this vague but perhaps crucial problem-solving technology, Engelbart recalled Bush's article, which he had read while he was stationed in the Phillipines.

Engelbart had been a radar operator in the Pacific, so he

knew you could present information to a person on a screen And by 1950 he was hearing things about these new devices called computers (there were only a few in existence at the time). Suddenly, the whole thing came to him—in an image, of course: Computers and screens could be used cooperatively by groups of people to create and use knowledge in order to solve complex problems. He saw a picture in his mind of a group of people in a theaterlike environment, pointing at screens and manipulating computers with knobs and dials. Little did he know that more than fifteen years would pass before that image emerged from his imagination and manifested in the form of a machine he could touch.

In 1963, having decided that he had to create an entirely new conceptual framework to understand the new way of using tools he had discovered, Engelbart published "A Conceptual Framework for the Augmentation of Man's Intellect," in which he proposed that highly graphic digital computers could be used to extend and amplify human thinking power. After more than a decade of theorizing in the wilderness of computer science, Engelbart was funded by the Defense Department's Advanced Research Projects Agency to the tune of a million dollars a year, from the late 1960s through the mid-1970s. The research laboratory he set up at the Stanford Research Institute was known as ARC (Augmentation Research Center). A team of inspired young *infonauts* set out to build his long-dreamed-of mind amplifier.

ARC's first goal was to create graphic displays for their computers. When graphic displays were created, the engineering team created devices whereby the computer user could command the machine by pointing to sensitive areas on the display screen—"pop-up menus," "icons," and "buttons." A whole new way of working with computers was constructed around the new, interactive, time-sharing computers and increasingly sophisticated video displays. The "mouse" pointing device, the use of a screen to display and manipulate text and graphics, the display of multiple windows of information, of displaying hierarchies of information and expanding or contracting the "view" of the hierarchy, computer-mediated conferences, multimedia meetings—almost all the hot "new" ideas of personal computer technology in the 1980s—originated as visions and prototypes in Engelbart's lab in the 1960s and 1970s.

The computers at ARC were designed to extend intellectual capabilities, but it wasn't possible in the 1960s to build a computer cheaply enough to devote to the use of a single person—until the miniaturization revolution went into high gear. In the early 1970s, a group of young computer designers, many of them veterans of Engelbart's laboratory, built the first personal computer, known as the "Alto," at Xerox Corporation's Palo Alto Research Center, known as PARC. Funded even more lavishly than ARC, equipped with state-of-the-art hardware, staffed with the cream of the young hardware designers, programmers, and computer scientists of the day, PARC was a utopia for the growing army of infonauts who had joined the quest for computer-assisted thinking tools. In the early 1980s, I interviewed several of the PARC veterans who had been in on the design of the Alto interface, and they recalled that the use of graphics to mediate between the human mind and the computer was at the core of their design philosophy.

The PARC computer builders had something the ARC team lacked, a new technology known as bit-mapped graphics. Every picture element on the screen is represented by a specific bit in the computer's memory—a "bit-map" that corresponds to the pattern of pixels on the screen. This technology made it possible for graphic representations as well as text to be displayed mosaic-style on the screen, by turning on and off the right patterns of pixels. This direct connection between the computer's memory and the user's visual system by way of the bit-mapped screen allows for a two-way interaction between human and computer: The computer can display menus, models, and messages to the user, and the user can point and click at an image on the screen and cause the computer to execute a string of commands. Instead of invoking a program by typing in its name, the user points at the program's icon and clicks the mouse.

By building vizthink tools into the user interface, the ARC and PARC designers fundamentally altered the way human minds and computers work together. *The representations of tools became the tools themselves:* Pointing at the text-editing icon and clicking the mouse is the same as opening the text editor with a command. Dragging the icon of a file to the trash-barrel icon will delete that file. In the mind of the user, the visual representation very quickly becomes the tool itself, which means the icons lined up on the periphery of a computer screen are externalized, visible, thinking tools. By glancing at the screen, it is possible to ascertain the date and time, note whether there is any incoming electronic mail waiting, see which projects have been left on the "electronic desktop" for immediate consideration, and look at the array of tools available.

Stuart Card, one of the Xerox designers I interviewed, recalled the day in the early 1970s when they finally got overlapping windows working on an Alto, and the work-surface seemed to "pop into the third dimension." The idea of "overlapping" objects on the screen, rather than arranging everything in a linear order, as had been necessary when computer input and output devices were teletypes rather then screens, was a key development in the evolution of graphic interfaces.

The whole idea of overlapping windows was to use the computer screen as an extension of human short-term memory in much the same way the objects on the surface of one's desk serve as an extension of memory. Although most people can remember an extraordinary amount of information in the long term, very few humans seem to be able to juggle more than around ten "chunks" of information in the short-term memory at the same time. In the 1950s, a psychologist by the name of George Miller quantified this peculiar deficiency in a research paper titled "The Magic Number Seven, Plus or Minus Two." There are two ways computers can get around this limitation: First, the screen can act as a visual cache, or extension, of the short-term memory; second, although the number of chunks is limited, it is possible to convey information in the very shape of the chunks, as in the instance of an icon that tells you whether the object is a document, a folder, or an executable program simply by conventional variations in its shape or shading.

The idea of a visual cache is not a new one. Blackboards and desktops serve the same purpose. If you are working on four or five projects, it helps to keep the papers visible on your desk instead of in a drawer as you sit in front of your desk. You are using the desktop and the papers as a visible cache for some short-term information, thus freeing a little space in your mental buffer. When you accumulate more pieces of paper, you might arrange them in stacks, and overlap them so that only the headlines are visible.

The desktop metaphor uses icons and buttons (visible, mouse-sensitive areas) on the screen as a way of reminding the computer user how to best use the computer. A blank screen is one of the most fiendish devices ever invented to torture new computer users who don't know whether their command saved their file or trashed it. By making key information about the computer's internal state available without asking in the form of graphics, the visual metaphor makes it easier to learn how to command the computer. Information is located by pointing and clicking on hierarchical browsers that automatically zero in on the sought-after text or graphic or program. The computer screen has become an intellectual workshop for the user, who doesn't have to learn arcane command syntax, but can learn by looking around. The first powerful vocabulary for visual thinking was the adoption of the desktop metaphor, which has spread like a meme from computer system to computer system. In a few years, virtually every personal computer in the world will use a visual language to communicate with users.

The direct manipulation interface pioneered by Engelbart and developed at PARC was unknown outside the rarefied heights of computer science for more than another decade. The idea wasn't unleashed on the world until somebody gave Steve Jobs of Apple Computer a tour of PARC. In 1984, the Apple Macintosh computer brought the graphic interface to the millions. And with the first Macintosh came the first publically accessible vizthink software—paint tools. With the advent of affordable computers like the Macintosh that people can use to create and control images on the screen and print them on paper, the visual empowerment of the general population became possible. Just as word processors and spreadsheets make it possible for people to write and analyze numerical information at a higher level because the computer takes care of lower-level tasks like moving paragraphs and recalculating equations, computer paint programs make it possible for people to think and communicate more easily with images by making it easier for them to represent their ideas visually.

The first mass-market computer drawing tool was Bill Atkinson's *Macpaint*, which was bundled with the first Macintosh computers in 1984. But computers have improved dramatically, and users have grown sophisticated and demanding since then. Second-generation paint programs and the introduction of page-layout programs, combined with the introduction of low-cost laser printers, have raised the art of computerized visual communication to a new level.

The several complementary technological elements of computer-assisted vizthink—the graphic interface, paint and layout programs, low-cost printers, are evolving rapidly enough to presume that by the end of this century, schoolchildren will carry devices as powerful as the most expensive desktop-publishing systems today. But two other powerful trends in computer technology are accelerating the spread of desktop vizthink: Inexpensive, high-capacity memory devices like optical disks are making it possible for individuals to carry very large amounts of visual information in their pockets. And digitizers—devices that convert optical images into computer-readable form—are creating inexpensive libraries of images that people are using to cut, paste, change, and exchange. By quickly browsing through a database of images, then mixing, matching, and manipulating them, it is possible for even the least "talented" computer user to put together effective visual presentations. Once an image is digitized, it can be copied in seconds, transmitted via phone lines, stored along with thousands of others for easy retrieval. Some of that daily vizblast can be filtered, culled, captured, and put to use in one's communications.

Personal-computer users are losing their fear of using graphics to communicate their thoughts. And that community is having a ripple effect on the whole culture. An increased emphasis on visual expression and visual thinking is already evident in documents and memos. In 1987, Bill Atkinson, one of the software fathers of the Macintosh, and the creator of Macpaint, loosed a new visual empowerment instrument on the world in the form of HyperCard, a visual programming tool that combines programming for non-programmers with powerful graphic capabilities. People are now beginning to exchange HyperCard-created "stacks" that contain animated graphics and sound as well as text and static images.

The evolving tool kit of graphic thought-amplifiers will undoubtedly have a synergistic effect on the development of vizthink curricula. The Macintosh has only been available since 1984. The first great masters of the new media are still learning their crafts. And those who will show us how to use the technology and the training to bootstrap our entire culture to a new way of thinking are the six-year-old infonauts of today who are growing up with this techno-social wave and who aren't being taught to believe you have to be an artist to educate your vision. It's possible that the daily visual life of our grandchildren will be as different from ours as ours differs from that of our grandparents (and will be, I hope, more coherent).

Nothing guarantees that vizthink will be an effective counter-measure to vizblast. And nothing guarantees that the social changes initiated by these new tools will all be beneficial. But it is possible that the new way of thinking could liberate us, as did the political revolutions of the eighteenth century and the literacy revolution of the seventeenth century. Which means that we can increase the odds of a positive outcome by envisioning it as clearly and communicably as possible.

Put down this book. Pick up a pencil. Start playing. The future might depend on it.

PART 4

MAGNETIC FIELDWORK

Bashed: What It's Like to Be in a Car Crash

Esther took her time saying good-bye. Judy decided to drive. I was in a hurry to get home, so I got in first and sat in back. We were driving through a quiet industrial district at eleven o'clock on a Saturday night, talking about what a nice evening it had been, when a large, dark vehicle came out of nowhere, jumped a stop sign and headed for *us*. Our reaction was . . . nothing. We simply refused to believe what our brains were telling us about the immediate future.

Then we all heard the squeal of skidding tires as Judy floored the brakes.

Next came a gut-punching slam as—yes—it happened. It was the kind of painful-sounding metallic smack that makes a person shudder in his bedroom two blocks away.

Finally, a crumple—not so loud as the slam but twice as sickening—as the exoskeleton of our vehicle gave way under the force of muscle car moving at seventy mph. Somewhere between the slam and the crumple was a higher-pitched counterpoint of splintering glass.

The other car took the crash head-on, mashing radiator-first into the driver's side of our car, from the fender to the wind-

191

shield. The impact spun our car into a fishtail, and we seemed to leave the ground as our mortally wounded Malibu swung around and counterbashed them broadside. The two traumatized automobiles were mysteriously welded together at this point, side by side. The concussion of the second collision sent a glass storm of shattered window particles through our car, but we were so intent on the unfolding event that nobody noticed the brief, sharp shower until later.

Two collisions, and the driver of the assaulting vehicle was still trying to get the hell out of there, vainly gunning his mangled engine, edging the two fused automobiles toward a brick wall. Judy was ramming the brake pedal to the floor with both feet, hanging on to the steering wheel with her left hand and trying to shove the gearshift into Park with her right. The other driver hampered our strategy by steering toward us at this point, in a last-ditch effort to avoid the brick wall and proceed down the street. Judy hit Reverse, jolting our bodies in an unhealthy manner and divorcing the two vehicles. We came to a stop. The other vehicle also came to a halt before it could smash into the brick wall—which was no surprise, since half its engine was embedded in our fender. The doors of the car flew open, and the four occupants jumped out and ran down the street without a backward glance.

I thought I smelled gasoline, although it turned out that none was leaking. The olfactory hallucinations came with the adrenaline afterblast. I shouted: "Everybody out! I smell gas!" All three of us squeezed out of what was left of the driver's side of the car. I knew that I was basically intact, and I asked if everyone else was OK. Judy and Esther both said *no* with such immediacy and conviction that I dragged them over to the streetlight for a look. "Head wounds bleed a lot," I said, impulsively drawing on the only experience I had with head wounds—television. I held Esther's shoulders and took a close-up look.

There was so much blood that at first I thought Esther's throat had been cut. Then I remembered the flying glass from the broadside collision. I checked her major neck arteries, saw that they were not the source of the bleeding, noted that her cheek was sort of hanging in space, but that her cheekbone was not exposed. Her eyes seemed to be intact, although incredibly bloodshot, and her eyebrows were dripping blood. By the time I'd checked this far, people from the neighborhood were running into the street. I handed Esther to the first person who came along and then turned to Judy. She had a dozen scratches on her cheeks, a few undecipherable scalp lacerations that were soaking the peach scarf I'd bought her at Bendel's and she was holding her neck with both hands. All three of us were spitting glass. We found our way into a Samaritan's van—thank you, Samaritan—and he ran all the red lights on the way to General Hospital.

Meanwhile, inside my body, a little gland not much larger than a walnut was keenly aware of the external developments. Electrochemical messages zipped back and forth between sense organs, midbrain, and emergency-action centers in the hypothalamus. The high command in the cortex gave the signal to create new neurohormones. Within milliseconds, the molecular message worked its way down the chain of command, until every organ and cell had been alerted to the unprecedented emergency status.

Deep in my gut, nestled above each kidney, another set of organs got the message. The good old adrenals started pumping those rare elixirs, adrenaline and noradrenaline. An instantaneous surge of muscular energy enabled me to brace my body with unaccustomed force. My emotions passed panic and went into overdrive. My body, it seemed, was going to take care of itself. That left my mind with a surprising amount of time to think.

The first slam didn't actually propel any glass into my body, but I *felt* the sound of a billion invisible shards penetrating every one of my nerve channels. A not unpleasant, but startling wave of heat followed the billion tiny electrodes into my overamped neurons. The senses of sound, sight, smell were all channeled into tactile sensation. It was as if the entire world had become *skin*, and along with the sudden sense of fragility came a curious, unexpected euphoria. For a peak millisecond or two, all the anxiety, pain, and raw panic of the collision was overshadowed by the ecstatic white light in my brain.

"This has to be the ultimate high," was one of the few thousand thoughts that ran through my mind while we were being bashed around. An involuntary, total-body overdrive is indeed a pure, intense, weirdly euphoric type of intoxicant. And it is available to everyone. You too can experience the sweet tingle and taste the primordial nectar of your own rushing adrenaline. All you need is the nerve to ride in an automobile.

There is one particularly distinct impression that still bubbles up at apparently random intervals. I can't say I saw it in the conventional sense, or even had time to think it, but the message was undeniable—a composite kiddy archetype with the face of Bugs Bunny and the voice of Porky Pig, stuttering: "Th-th-that's *all* folks!" as I prepared to depart the world to this last *Looney Tunes*. Disney Bardo. The crack between the worlds. Except I didn't fade to black—not in this alternate world; instead, I stayed wide awake, flashing mightily.

Time became deliciously colloidal, like those slo-mo, gooey-lens scenes in tearjerker television movies. The sound of squealing tires triggered an internal time sludgifier, which slowed everything down for agonizing perusal. There was time to think, even to meditate, in those complex seconds before metal met metal. "Is this what our lives add up to?" was one of the more prominent questions. As was the ever-urgent "Why me?"

If we had lingered a second longer before we started our car, we might have been the bashers instead of the bashees, and the four felons who fled into the night would have been picking glass out of their faces. If we had arrived a fraction of a second earlier, we might have avoided the accident or, more likely, the bashing would have happened full broadside and they would still be washing us off the pavement.

I can't say that I've ever seen my life passing in front of my eyes, but the sound of crunching metal did pull a dozen detailed files out of my memory banks. There was the very first time the distinctive squeal-slam-crumple sound track was revealed to me: I was sixteen, newly licensed to drive a tiny Renault around the streets of Phoenix, Arizona, hired to deliver brushes to bouffanted housewives and hoping vainly to be seduced by one of them.

I wasn't yet aware that the laws of traffic and the habits of humans don't always agree. Someone ignored a stop sign, and I ended up with my entire body ingeniously folded in the only uncrunched area of my Renault, where the passenger would have put his legs. The radio speaker was jolted out of the dashboard and dangled in front of my face, blasting out a golden oldie, the title of which still eludes me.

Another memory—this one from somebody else's wreck— came to me when the first impact spun our car around for the broadside slam. Over ten years ago, two psychic desperados of my acquaintance decided to drive from Portland, Oregon, to New York City, using LSD to keep them awake. Somewhere in Wyoming, they made a wrong decision and wrapped their car around a tree.

They sat there, physically uninjured, cosmically baffled, hallucinating insanely. Eventually one of them turned to the other and whispered, "Know where we can score some more adrenaline?" That quote, and the look on the face of the survivor as he told it to me, floated up a decade later, when my own glandular floodgates dumped every milliliter of joy juice my adrenals could muster into my frantically pumping circulatory system.

It must be noted that adrenaline is the oldest form of intoxication known to man or beast. It's the billion-year-old high, the original fight-or-flight fuel. Awareness is a command-and-control setup for our biological defense systems: We can see danger; we can hear danger; we can grab danger by the god-damn throat and throttle it until it isn't dangerous anymore.

It's been noted before, but it still comes as a surprise: There is no immediate pain; *that* comes later, when you're lying under megacandle light in the emergency ward. Instead, there is a peculiar sense of aliveness that comes over you when all your dormant defenses turn themselves up to the last notch on the internal control panel. I was later to learn that the billion elec-trodes that pleasurably penetrated my nerves were really a net-work of capillaries bursting under an adrenaline-charged blood rush. The doctor in the emergency ward warned me that my body would be very sore all over for a few days, because the adrenaline rush shot so much blood through my system that the capillaries didn't have time to expand to accommodate the flow.

The day after the accident, my own doctor told me that my left shoulder felt crucified *not* because I hit it against anything tangible, but because my own muscles braced for the collision with such force that I tore something. The adrenal hormones had liberated the huge stash of glucose in my liver and unlocked the reserves of free fatty acids in my muscles, giving me the momentary power to wreck myself. After a decade of responsi-ble drug abuse, it was appalling to realize that a couple of drops of stuff from two lumps above my kidneys could induce me to do what assorted stimulants, hallucinogens, animal tran-quilizers, and vodka had failed to accomplish. You can live an entire lifetime without ever getting so excited that you break something inside your own body. Unless, of course, you get bashed.

The Ultimate Cashflow

Billions of dollars used to pass through my hands every day. Frankly, I enjoyed it.

I liked my job so much that I sometimes arrived early in order to admire the building where I did my business. That black marble monument to money, the Bank of America world headquarters in San Francisco, is probably the most widely disdained structure in town. I can't think of a single friend or acquaintance who doesn't have a few derogatory opinions to express about my former office. A few bold locals might cop to a grudging fondness for the Transamerica period, but natives agree that the monolith is, in essence, a rude gesture. One friend explained his feelings: "Those guys at the top aren't concerned about our view. They put fifty stories of stone up there without bothering to consult you or me because they hold the cards and we don't."

Perhaps he is right, but I still find a cool, inhuman beauty in the place. A.P. Giannini Plaza is also mocked as a quarter-block concrete concession to the humans who inhabit the neighborhood. There is a tiny plot of grass, a great square of brick, flowers in enormous stone bowls that only a madman in a cargo

197

helicopter could steal. There is also a sculpture in the plaza, a chunk of polished rock even blacker than the mother structure above it. Sharp-edged, as massive and immobile as the giant planters, it is widely known as Banker's Heart. I'm growing fond of it as well.

Once or twice a week I sat near the monstrous flower bowls to watch the people and the buildings. I still stop there whenever I'm in the neighborhood. The shadows of the monolith sometimes create a ziggurat against the fog; on sunny days, its silhouette slices a serrated chunk of black from the blue sky.

Banker's Heart is only forty-five seconds away from my former battle station on the eleventh floor. The moment I stepped through the door of my office I journeyed into the center of a sensory storm. In a large, flourescent-irradiated chamber, forty-odd people moved efficiently among business machines and file cabinets. Visitors adjusted quickly to the harsh, shadowless lighting, but it was impossible to escape the sound, the incredible din of money on the move.

Technology has encroached upon financial acoustics since my tenure in the wire room, but the sound of money when I worked there was one that most people would find vaguely familiar. It wasn't the crisp riffling of fresh currency or the happy ringing of cash registers. Next time you watch the news on television, pay attention to the teletype sound in the background before it fades into the face of the newscaster. Most newsrooms have silent terminals rather than clattering teletypes nowadays, but that mechanical din is still used as a reminder of the way journalism used to sound. That clatter, multiplied a hundredfold, is the sound money makes in those parts of the banking world that haven't computerized their wire rooms yet.

In teletype rooms from Bombay to Indianapolis, money still comes chattering off the wires at 210 words per minute, spewing out fanfolds of wide white printout paper and curling mountains of narrow yellow punched tape.

Ten years ago, I was a teletype operator at Central Telegraph, an obsolescent human bottleneck in the financial intercourse of nations. Teletype operators were replaced at the Bank of America by sleek consoles full of silicon and circuitry, so my coworkers and I were the last of the human money movers. To a teletype operator of the old school, money is nothing more nor less than a message, a message one banker sends to another. That part hasn't changed—only the communication technology is different.

Teletype was the most economical way to transmit written messages, until low-cost computers came along, and banking tends to generate a lot of written messages, twenty-four hours a day in a dozen languages, to and from every country that rates a place on the map. Teletype machines are archaic-looking and rather loud. Stock tickers are their more muted cousins. Think of those old movies where tuxedoed tycoons stared out the windows of their penthouses, idly fingering the tape as it emerged from the glass-housed ticker to coil politely into a tasteful wastebasket. Bankwire machines are much more hefty items, about the size of a small desk, and when you are in the same room with a hundred of them, the sound level is like an eternal replay of a million knitting needles falling onto a tin roof.

While my colleagues and I processed paper, hour by hour, we couldn't help reading the messages as we marked, folded, coiled, stapled, and filed. The messages processed in a typical shift might include a $150 million bank syndication financing Mexico's sugar crop; $900,000 in the form of potatoes, a transaction requiring sixteen documents certifying the absence of specific insects and fungi and an affidavit from the captain confirming that they were shipped at a temperature of 4 to 6 degrees Celsius and humidity of 85 percent; bank transfers between Reykjavik and Gambia, Beijing and Toronto, Phoenix and Minneapolis; messages about messages, inquiring if last night's wire said $6,000 or $6 million (for potatoes, armaments, tractors, pantyhose); arrangements for the movement of bank personnel bearing exotic names to and from exotic places; $162 million communication satellite systems for Indonesia; two executive jets for the Bangladesh government; $150 to Janie Doe in Pago Pago, "write soon, love, Mom."

The executive jets for Bangladesh struck me as rather incongruous, I remember, since it is probably the poorest country in the world. They are so poor that they receive foreign aid from India—and it can't be more than a day's train ride across the entire country. The transactions involving the People's Republic of China or Poland or the Soviet Union also threw me a bit at first. I had always envisioned a state of economic warfare between capitalist and socialist nations, but come to think of it, there must be some kind of banking involved when Russia buys U.S. grain or when China buys farm machinery from Canada. Bankers move money beyond, around, or despite boundaries of nationality or ideology. Those aren't tons of dollar bills or rubles or yen being bandied about by all the feverish communicating—those are tons of food, clothing, medicine, and armaments.

A teletype operator must monitor a hundred minor details of method and machinery, but the process quickly becomes semiautomatic. Money moves in cycles, pulsing between trickle and torrent as shifts change and banks open around the world; at peak traffic hours it took two fast operators to keep the incoming paper from burying the receiving machines, and a dozen more to retransmit. The tape constantly piled up and snaked across the floor, to be processed and sent out again, creating rivers of paper tape for the operators at the other ends of the lines. Tapes and paper rolls were changed rapidly, like pit stops on an endless road race. After a while, I caught the feel of gigantic economic tempos, literally sensing the pulse of international trade through my fingertips.

The names at the bottom of the wires reveal a lot about the business of international banking. There is a consistent matching of names to territory. If there is a banking problem in Saudi Arabia, then the name of the person in charge of solving it is something like Khaled Gebesh. José Bejarano handles South American troubleshooting. Lu for Asia, Feldman for Israel, Haramoto for Japan. It's more hardboiled than equal opportunity hiring; the whole business illustrates something about the true nature of multinational corporations, about the subordination of personal and national loyalty to the sheer celebration of transaction, the ritual transference of wealth from one place to another and back again.

Charisma has gone the way of pocket watches and sleeve garters. The entire ambiance of banking has changed. A friend of mine who washes windows outside highrise offices told me that window washers refer to the people inside the buildings as drones. There is, indeed, a distinct flavor of hive life in the new buildings, from the illogically hexagonal offices to the identical carpeted hallways. In the old days, banks weren't hives—they were temples.

From the east side of the monolith one can look down on the roof of the old headquarters on Montgomery Street. There is a peculiar structure on the roof, one that probably wasn't built to be gazed on from above. There is an actual temple up there, hardly visible from the street, with fluted white marble pillars and carved lintels, and a tiny second temple on top, domed, the corroded green of ancient copper: a monument to the era when money moved at a more gentlemanly pace. I think those temples are maintained as a haven for the restless spirits of old bankers, those archaic creatures who dealt in gold and handwritten drafts, who handled wealth that could be touched and lifted and kept in vaults.

Virtual Communities

WHAT'S VIRTUAL ABOUT A COMMUNITY?

Because I'm a writer, I spend a lot of time alone with my words and thoughts. After work, I reenter the human community via my neighborhood, my family, my circle of personal and professional acquaintances. Until recently, I often felt isolated and lonely during the working day, and my work provided few opportunities to expand my circle of friends and colleagues. For the past three years, however, I have participated in a wide-ranging, intellectually stimulating, professionally rewarding, and often intensely emotional exchange with dozens of new friends and hundreds of colleagues. And I still spend my days in an office, physically isolated. My mind, however, is linked with a worldwide collection of like-minded (and not so like-minded) souls: my virtual community.

A virtual community is as real as any other web of communications, memories, meetings, and alliances that links a group of people. It is "virtual" in the sense that the medium of communication is a network of computers connected through telephone lines. These communities can include, but do not depend on, any physical gathering of bodies at the local well, town square, or downtown bar. The elimination of physical proximity as a criterion for community portends radical changes in the way we live. This kind of cultural transformation is an old story: From the first bands of hunter-gatherers on the prehistoric savanna to the swarms of minds in today's global communications network, communities are created when people exchange information with one another and about one another.

My community is a place I visit for the sheer pleasure of communicating with my friends, and a practical instrument I use to scan and gather information on subjects of momentary or enduring importance to my work or my life, from childcare to neuroscience, from technical questions on telecommunications to arguments on philosophical, political, or spiritual subjects. It's a bit like a neighborhood pub or coffee shop: There are old buddies and delightful newcomers and new tools waiting, and fresh graffiti and mail, except instead of shutting down the computer and walking to the corner to join my comrades, I just invoke my telecom program and *voilà*—there they are. It's a place. It's a little like a salon, where I can participate in a hundred ongoing conversations with people who don't care what I look like or sound like, but who do care how I think and communicate. And it's a little like a groupmind, where questions are answered, support is given, inspiration is provided, by people I may never have heard from before, and whom I may never meet face to face.

The new kinds of communities differ from previous communities in one crucial respect: The human species has never before used a communication device that is able to show people *who* to communicate with. For me, the way groups of people use these intelligent communication tools to weave friendships out of the evanescent transactions of digital messages has been one of the strongest demonstrations of true magic I've ever experienced. It's not the kind of magic you do with spells or smoke and mirrors. It's the magic that always has impelled people to create better and better ways to make contact with one another and to build communities together.

With each technological step in the evolution of communication tools, people find that they can communicate with many more people than had previously been possible and soon discover that they also *wanted* to communicate with many of those people. Language, alphabetic writing, the printing press, the telephone network, radio, and television each changed and expanded the definition of "community" because of the unique new ways each new medium could connect people to one another. Computer-mediated communications are the latest step in the coevolution of communities and communication technologies, and the appearance of thousands of virtual communities in the late 1980s is a harbinger of changes to come in the way people deal with each other on a daily basis.

It sounds like science fiction to people who haven't participated in it, but the use of computer conferencing and electronic mail as social media as well as business tools is soaking its way into American culture: Today, as you walk down the street, sit in your office, enter your classroom, you can be sure that one or two of the people around you don't go to a bar or a bowling alley after work but boot up their computers instead, turn on their modems, and shmooze with their buddies at one of the nodes of the Worldnet.

I stumbled into virtual communication space a couple years after I switched from a typewriter to a word processor. One day, because an editor wanted me to send her drafts of my manuscript by electronic mail, I discovered that the computer I had been using exclusively for word processing and games had the power to reach out through my telephone and find exactly the right people to communicate with. That feature immediately changed the way I deal with people and had an even greater impact on the way I find and choose people to deal with. A virtual community isn't an abstraction to me when I encounter the new people in my life whom I didn't know a couple of years ago, and whom I never would have met if I hadn't tapped into the online realm. And where else but the virtual community could I have dealt with Clyde Ghost Monster, the Covenant of the Goddess, and an advisory panel of the U.S. Congress?

Individual members of virtual communities may or may not ever meet one another face to face, although they regularly and familiarly exchange information and innuendo, jokes and ideas. Like any other community, they are also collections of people who adhere to certain (loose) social contracts and who share certain (eclectic) interests. It usually has a geographically local focus and often has a connection to a much wider domain. The local focus of my virtual community, the *Whole Earth 'Lectronic Link* (aka the Well) is the San Francisco Bay Area; the wider locus consists of thousands of other computer communities around the world and hundreds of thousands of other communitarians, linked via exchanges of messages into a meta-community known as the Usenet. Part Global Village, part Homo Gestalt.

To a small group of planners, communicators, and technologists in government and various research institutes, virtual communities have been a way of life for more than a decade. Originally, they were called "online communities," and it was foreseen that they would show up in the real world when people could afford to have powerful computers on their desktops. By virtue of word processing and electronic spreadsheets, increasingly powerful computers have indeed populated our offices and more than a few of our homes. The cost of computation has dropped dramatically enough by the late 1980s, and the communication infrastructure has become densely and globally interconnected enough, for online communities to begin expanding to include many more people outside the community of specialists.

The existence of today's computer-linked communities was predicted twenty years ago by J.C.R. Licklider, who set in motion the research that resulted in the creation of the first such community, the ARPAnet: "What will on-line interactive communities be like?" Licklider wrote in 1968, in an article on "The Computer As a Communication Device." "In most fields they will consist of geographically separated members, sometimes grouped in small clusters and sometimes working individually. They will be communities not of common location but of common interest."

My friends and I are part of the future that Licklider dreamed about, and we can attest to the truth of his prediction that "life will be happier for the on-line individual because the people with whom one interacts most strongly will be selected more by commonality of interests and goals than by accidents of proximity." At this moment, thousands of people—communicators, organizers, teenagers, housewives, college students, military officers, scientists, techies, witches, teachers, quadriplegics, stockbrokers, retired people—are meeting others who share a passion for cetaceans or an interest in Welsh music, even though the others may be hundreds of miles away.

Although only a small percentage of the population currently takes part in computer conferencing, this mode of communication and community-building is almost twenty years old. It took several hardware and software revolutions, a few colliding ideas, and a thousand infonauts test-piloting the first generations of inner-space devices to get where we are today. The technical and social constraints that have confined the use of this mind-tool to a small group of enthusiasts are rapidly disappearing. Judging from the current rate of growth in computer and communications technology, the telecommunicating subculture will probably expand to a much larger portion of the population over the next ten years, just as personal computers did, ten years ago.

The history of this new metamedium winds a serendipitous course from the bowels of the Pentagon to the bedrooms of teenage hobbyists. In order to understand the future of computer-linked communities, it helps to know where they originated and how they evolved. I'll trace this history a little later, but first I want to show you a small sample of what life is like today among the online set.

A DIP INTO THE WELL

Here's a glimpse of what a brief visit to the Well looks like from my point of view. First, my desktop computer uses an electronic device known as a modem to connect me, via one of my two telephone lines (all telecommunication addicts have two telephone lines), with a more powerful computer, located several miles from my home. Except for the size of my phone bill, it doesn't matter whether the remote computer is down the block or in another hemisphere. It could be an inexpensive personal computer in a teenager's bedroom, or a state-of-the-art mainframe at a university or government installation. My modem and the remote computer's modem speak to each other over the same phone lines I use to call my Aunt Florence; my modem uses electronic beeps and boops to convey to the remote computer, by means of a code of audible tones, the words I type on my desktop computer keyboard.

Although a certain number of programs are executed in my personal computer and in the remote computer, I'm not programming but communicating. That is, the bulk of my transactions with the computer network consists of words: messages I send to other people on a person-to-person basis; messages I narrowcast to a small mailgroup or conference or broadcast to all those who want to read them; messages I have gathered or have been sent from other virtual communitarians. The computer helps us pass those words around in a structured manner In the following list, think of each conference as a kind of room where people go to talk about various aspects of the topic that is listed on the door. Each menu item is a door, and the words in parentheses after the name of each conference are the key:

CONFERENCES ON THE WELL

Best of the WELL (g best)

Business—Education

Business	(g biz)	Calendar	(g cal)
Classifieds	(g cla)	Consumers	(g cons)
Desktop Publishing	(g desk)	Education	(g ed)
Legal	(g legal)	Library	(g lib)
Stock Market	(g stock)	One-Person Business	(g one)
The Future	(g fut)	Success	(g suc)
Work	(g work)	Word Processing	(g word)

Social—Political—Humanities

Aging	(g age)	Archives	(g arc)
Curious ?'s	(g que)	Drugs	(g dru)
Environment	(g env)	Gay	(g gay)
Health	(g heal)	In Context	(g context)
Islam	(g isl)	Jewish	(g jew)
Languages	(g lang)	Liberty	(g liberty)
Mind	(g mind)	Men on the WELL	* (g mow)
Nonprofits	(g non)	Parenting	(g par)
Peace	(g pea)	Poetry	(g poetry)

*Private conference—mail mo for entry

Philosophy	(g phi)	Politics	(g pol)
Psychology	(g psy)	Rainbow	(g rain)
Role-Playing Games	(g rpg)	Sexuality	(g sex)
Spirituality	(g spi)	True Confessions	(g tru)
User Interface	(g inter)	Words	(g words)
Whole Earth Symposium	(g wes)	Women on the WELL	*(g wow)
Writers	(g wri)		

Arts—Recreation—Entertainment

ArtCom Electronic Net	(g acen)	Audio-Videophilia	(g aud)
Art Directions	(g art)	Comics	(g comics)
Cooking	(g cook)	Corner Pub	(g pub)
Eating	(g eat)	Fine Arts	(g fine)
Games	(g games)	Gardening	(g gard)
Grateful Dead	(g gd)	Jokes	(g jokes)
MIDI	(g midi)	Movies	(g movies)
Motorcycling	(g ride)	Music	(g mus)
On the Air	(g ota)	Outdoors	(g out)
Rasslin'	(g ras)	Science Fiction	(g sf)
Sports	(g spo)	Television	(g tv)

Computers

AI	(g ai)	Amiga	(g amiga)
Apple & Dtack	(g app)	Atari	(g ata)
Big Computers	(g big)	BMUGSIG	(g bmug)
Commodore	(g com)	Computer Books	(g cbook)
Computer Graphics	(g gra)	CP/M	(g cpm)
Databasics	(g dat)	Enable	(g ena)
Fido	(g fido)	Forth	(g forth)

*Private conference—mail sof for entry

Framework	(g fra)	Homebrew/Hackers	(g home)
IBM PC	(g ibm)	Kaypro	(g kay)
Laptop	(g lap)	Macintosh	(g mac)
MicroPro	(g mic)	Microtimes	(g microx)
Programmer's Net	(g net)	Unix	(g unix)

Technical—Communications

Electronics	(g ele)	Home Repair	(g rep)
Info	(g boing)	Packet Radio	(g pac)
Photography	(g pho)	Science	(g science)
Space	(g spa)	Technical Writers	(g tec)
Telecommunications	(g tele)	Video	(g vid)

The WELL Itself

Entry	(g ent)	General	(g gen)
Help	(g help)	Hosts	(g hosts)
Manual	(g manual)	System News	(g news)

As you might surmise from this eclectic list, the Well actually consists of many communities that partially overlap with one another. Every Well subscriber visits from one to a dozen or more conferences every day or every week, from minutes to hours at a stretch. The population of the community is around two thousand at the moment, growing at the rate of two or three new members every day. Each of these conferences may be visited by a hundred or more people each day. Every conference has a "host" who sets the tone, makes people feel welcome, and helps people learn their way around.

The next excerpt from my Well session shows how I open the door of the Mind Conference, then type a command that shows me all the topics within the conference. If each conference can be seen as a kind of virtual room where people go to discuss a specific interest area, then each topic within a conference can be thought of as a conversation on an aspect of that interest area. The topics can be visualized as a series of electronic blackboards around the room. Anybody can enter the room, choose a blackboard, read what people have written on that blackboard, and add a comment at the bottom for others to read.

Here is what the list of the Mind Conference's topics looked like recently. The number on the far left helps you find your way to the topic.

Welcome to the Mind Conference

Type "browse" to see a list of topics

Ok (? for help): browse

item nresp header

1	41	The Information Processing Model: Computation as a Probe of Cognition
2	47	Neuroscience: Hardware, Wetware, and Software
3	101	Dreams and Dreamwork: Experiments in the Other Dimension
4	41	Other corners of the mind
5	128	Shady's place—Q and A with a cosmic Entity
6	57	Mind and Music
7	85	Word Viruses
8	64	intuition in business
9	46	Speechless
10	77	MIND GAME 1 (MG1)—A Multiplayer Treasure Hunt

The second number indicates the number of responses (consecutive entries on the topic's blackboard) that have been posted since the topic was opened. The first thing you might want to do is read all the responses in the topic about "Favorite States of Consciousness." By issuing a command to "Read #29," you will be able to see the following excerpt of the first few responses in that topic:

Topic 29: Favorite states of consciousness.
By: Howard Rheingold (hlr) on Wed, Nov 5, '86
38 responses so far

One of my favorite states of consciousness is the one that blissfully clicks on when you awaken from a bad dream. "Oh, *this* is real and *that* is not! Whew!" And I imagine (but don't know, of course) that enlightenment must feel something like that. Are there any *other* favorite, unusual, intense, joyful, terrible, weird, describable states of mind that you'd care to talk about?

38 responses total.

Topic 29: Favorite states of consciousness.

1: Don Pelton (dep) Wed, Nov 5, '86 (16:51)

About the dream: Stephen LaBerge, in his work on lucid dreaming, suggests that a potent induction technique is to ask yourself, throughout your day, from time to time, in your ordinary waking state. . . . "Am I dreaming?" The effect of doing this practice for a few days, lucid dreams or not, is quite strange.

2: Tom Mandel (mandel) Wed, Nov 5, '86 (17:08)

Another one I like a lot is a state of mind that I can best describe as half-awake and half-dreaming. It happens sometimes before I fall fully asleep and sometimes just as I'm waking, especially if I'm waking out of a heavy dream. It's sort of like being semi-plugged into two worlds, the world of my mind and the external world around me. It's a state I rarely feel that I want to leave . . . but then Alex Bennett starts shouting at me from the radio.

(Actually, my earliest clear recollection of this state occurred one Sunday morning a year ago, when I had apparently left the clock-radio alarm on. I seemed to enter this very strange dream that started out with "May I see your passport, please?" This dream went on for twenty minutes or so before I realized that I was in fact listening to a radio program. Boy, I didn't know whether to laugh or cry when it was over. (This was, as it turns out, my first experience with the wonderful Firesign Theatre, of which I have since become a devoted follower.)

#3: Robin G. Ramsey (robngail) Wed, Nov 5, '86 (17:52)

I also enjoy the half-and-half state (half asleep, half awake). Awake enough to enjoy how good it feels to be dozing, awake enough to be aware I'm dreaming, sometimes incorporating outside voices, conversations, noises into my dreams . . . very much of a floating feeling.

4: Mary Eisenhart (marye) Wed, Nov 5, '86 (18:03)

What's most striking about that state, as far as I'm concerned, is having dreams which you are ACTUALLY WATCHING HAPPEN, just as in waking reality, and then when you finally do wake up it takes a lot of convincing to make you realize it didn't really happen. People coming in and out of the room when you live by yourself, conversations when nobody's there, etc.

5: Jef Poskanzer (pokey) Wed, Nov 5, '86 (19:56)

Listening to the Firesign Theatre is a worthwhile state of mind by itself.

My favorite state of mind is when I get so in tune with a program I'm working on that I can IMMEDIATELY diagnose a bug and visualize the fix. And what's really fun is when I do this for a program I've never even looked inside of, and when I go to put in the fix I just dreamed up, the code is exactly the way I pictured it.

6: Howard Rheingold (hlr) Thu, Nov 6, '86 (08:07)

The state that occurs when you are physiologically asleep but are aware that you are dreaming is "lucidity" and the state halfway between sleeping and waking is known as the "hypnopompic" state. Elmer and Alyce Green of the Menninger Foundation conducted a lot of psychophysiological research and found similarities between hypnopompic phenomena and those that manifest during theta training (theta is when your brainwaves slow down below the alpha range of 8–12 cps. I think theta is around 4–6 cps.) Robert Louis Stevenson used to allow a whole workshop of dream "brownies" to compose stories for him. He kept himself in a hypnopompic state by propping his arm up so his hand was pointing straight up, balanced on his elbow. He could comfortably drift around theta in this pose, but if he fell into a deeper sleep his hand would fall and wake him up. He tells the story of how Jekyll and Hyde was written this way in "An Essay on Dreams."

7: Ramon Sender Barayon (rabar) Thu, Nov 6, '86 (09:32)

Some yogis achieve R.L. Stevenson's results by tying a strand of hair to the tree branch under where they are seated. If they nod off, the tug on the strand brings them back.

8: David Taylor (elm) Sat, Nov 8, '86 (12:26)

Another nice state of mind: I was driving back from a wonderful evening up in the city last Tuesday and suddenly realized that I have a great life! I just started smiling uncontrollably and laughing, while driving down 280 at 70 or so, 1:30 in the morning. I've had that a few times in the last month or so.

9: Jef Poskanzer (pokey) Sat, Nov 8, '86 (21:09)

(Dave: Don't worry, you can be cured.)

Note that the topic was opened on a Wednesday, and the last quoted response took place the following Saturday. Conference topics are asynchronous—although you can read it in a few minutes, the "conversation" actually took place over a period of days and might well be continuing on at this moment, years after it first started. A hot topic might accumulate a hundred responses in a matter of hours. Another topic might go on for years before it hits fifty responses. This topic is like many in that it mixes serious infomation with a bit of joking. In virtual communities, the joking can be as informationally useful as the hard information, for it gives people a chance to get to know one another and remind each other that they are people, not just disembodied minds.

Similar conference structures will undoubtedly continue to exist and evolve for those purposes where words on a screen serve a purpose. With the advent of new technologies in the 1990s and beyond, it will be possible for people to add voice messages and graphics (eventually, even high-resolution color and motion, indistinguishable from high-resolution television images) to their responses. Certain sites on today's version of the ARPAnet are already experimenting with multimedia conferencing. Where it goes is anybody's guess. And a lot of forecasters in government and industry are trying their best to make informed guesses about the opportunities and pitfalls that will accompany the communication revolution of the 1990s.

Before one can predict the future of any communication medium with any hope of accuracy, it pays to look at the origins of that medium. In the case of computer conferencing, the plot turns out to be considerably thicker than the story of the origins of the telephone or television.

HOW DID WE GET HERE FROM THERE?

Some inventions make life more convenient or free people from onerous labor. Other inventions can change the way people think, often in ways the inventors never anticipated. A century after the invention of moveable type, the literate community in Europe had grown from a privileged minority to a substantial proportion of the population. With the growth of a community of readers and writers, the printed page became a medium for the propagation of ideas about chemistry and poetry, evolution and revolution, democracy and psychology, technology and industry, and other notions far beyond the ken of the people who invented movable type and started cranking out Bibles.

Computer conferencing came from several unexpected sources—the Berlin airlift of 1948, the vision of a man in California who wanted to use machines to amplify people's ability to solve problems, the unorthodox computer wizards around the country who liked to talk with one another via their computers in the late 1960s, and the wage-price freeze of 1971. Community communication was first attempted during the Berlin blockade and airlift, when the only agency that had direct real-time communication channels of its own to all the NATO countries was the State Department, with its old-style teletype machines.

Somebody tried to wire all the machines together without computers to organize the message stream, and found out that the problem is more complicated than that.

One of the first people to recognize the potential of the computer as a communication tool was Doug Engelbart, a researcher at Stanford Research Institute who has been working since the early 1960s on a scheme to use computers for "augmenting human intellect." Engelbart's Augmentation Research Center created many of the first tools for group communications via computer and later became the "librarians" of the ARPAnet, the first computer network. The ARPAnet itself was the result of a mini-revolution in computer technology, spearheaded by small groups of unorthodox, visionary, somewhat idiosyncratic computer programmers scattered among computer labs around the country.

In the early 1960s, J.C.R. Licklider, the fellow who made the predictions about online communities of the future quoted earlier in this essay, was in charge of the Information Processing Office of the Advanced Research Projects Agency (aka ARPA). He decided that computer technology was the basis of *all* future technologies, defense-related and otherwise, and put his support behind all those who believed computers could be made more powerful, cheaper, and easier to use than the mainframes of the 1950s.

It turned out that a lot of the programmers who helped create the ARPA-sponsored technologies were teenage dropout geniuses who created their own subculture, called themselves "hackers," and built new ways to use computers as instruments of thought rather than as giant calculators. Licklider, his more orthodox researchers, and the hackers shared the same wish: to break the technical barrier that prevented computer-system builders from interacting directly with their computers. Licklider's disciples, converted to his vision of "interactive computing" using keyboards and televisionlike CRT screens instead of punched cards and printouts, spent the 1960s creating the hardware and software necessary to manifest this vision. When their efforts began to succeed, the result was called "time sharing." Instead of supplying batches of cards to the central computer's administrator, programmers could plug into the computer directly, all at the same time, by using keyboard-and-screen "terminals" to interact with the computer.

A funny thing happened when groups of programmers found themselves sharing the same computer. They invented ways to communicate with one another, using the computer. The hackers wanted to exchange programming code, pass messages, debate politics or chess, or share phone numbers of take-out Chinese food restaurants that were open all night. And they wanted to do all this without leaving their computer terminals. Thus was the first prototype "electronic mail" system born.

It became obvious to Licklider that all these bright young researchers in Massachusetts, Utah, California, and elsewhere ought to be in touch with one another. More importantly, he saw that the software and hardware resources that had been developed at these separate sites ought to be linked together. In the early 1970s, the ARPAnet was created: a combination of hardware and software that could communicate computer information over common-carrier channels and thus enable geographically remote computers to share information and even programs. When the system was put into place, the people who had been sharing electronic mail messages over their local systems found that they were plugged into a nationwide network, an exciting new kind of community.

At about the same time that this group of computer scientists and programmers around the country were trying to put together ARPAnet, a fellow named Murray Turoff was working on computer-based simulations for a Washington, D.C., think tank. Some of these games involved connecting several "players" at once, via remote computing systems. As a result of this experience, Turoff became interested in using computers to mediate a process known as the "Delphi method," in which printed questionnaires and responses are circulated among a community of experts in order to find creative solutions to complex problems. Turoff thought the process was ideally suited to the kind of online communications that were then being developed on the ARPAnet. So he started to experiment with a computerized Delphi system.

In the early 1970s, Turoff had moved to the Office of Emergency Preparedness, where his job wasn't related to his interests in teleconferencing. But then came the wage-price freeze of 1971, an action that required the rapid collection, collation, and dissemination of an unprecedent amount of information. Turoff's superiors changed their minds about the value of his "extracurricular" experiments. The EMISARI (Emergency Management Information System and Reference Index) system was ready for action just in time. In the process of putting it together, the people who designed the system and the people who used it began to discover that some of its features seemed to become popular with the online community with no official urging. They were discovering what today's technological forecasters are recognizing as a general principle: Given a new communication medium, people will find unplanned unauthorized uses for it, out of sheer love of communication.

For the small community of people who had access to such systems in the 1970s, the continuing dialogues on computer science and foreign policy, space shuttles and video games, diatribes, puns, puzzles, gossip, criticism, pranks, and running jokes grew as important as the programming tasks for which the systems had been designed. The use of computers as a communication metamedium seemed to foster a certain set of values. Iconoclasm, debate, the expression of strong opinions, and the right to an unbridled heterogeneity of interests seemed to be highly valued in the online community.

*　　　*　　　*

BBS POPULISM

The original online communities were confined to an elite population of users during the 1960s and 1970s because it took a lot of expensive computing power to run a network. But in 1978, a grassroots effort by personal computer hobbyists started what might be called the "populist" phase of computer communications—the era of the bedroom bulletin-board system. Ward Christensen and Randy Seuss set up the first personal computer bulletin-board system (BBS) in Chicago in 1978, and ten years later the number of BBSs is in the tens of thousands, with a combined user population of hundreds of thousands. All it requires to create your own virtual community is a personal computer, a modem, and a BBS program. By leaving such a computer-and-telephone system hooked up all night or around the clock and posting the access number on one or two other BBSs, the grapevine takes care of the rest. It's a little like a mushroom farm: Set it up, go away, and by the next morning, a community has started to create itself.

The first months of my exploration of bulletin boards were like a series of electronic anthropology field trips. For a couple of hours every night or two, over a period of several months, I discovered that the diversity of different communities was already beyond anyone's power to track or control. I encountered teenage philosophers, homespun lecturers of all ages and both sexes who were willing to ramble about any topic you'd care to name, and I even stumbled onto a couple of online religions, both cybernetic and neopagan. The folkways of a whole culture had been worked out in millions of online conversations by the time I delved into the BBS realm in the early 1980s.

I met Clyde Ghost Monster one night out in the bulletin-board zone, and Clyde turned me on to my first online religion. It started the way it often does when you browse the boards. A list of bulletin-board numbers led me to a BBS called Sunrise, consisting of random drop-ins from several different parts of the country, like me, and a core group, mostly local, who seemed to know each other. Sunrise appeared to be a hybrid of an electronic cracker-barrel store and a public toilet wall. I didn't learn for several weeks that Clyde is a seventeen-year-old girl. She told me to try a BBS closer to home, in Santa Cruz, and look at the topic labeled "Origins."

FELLOWSHIP   PRACTICE   TRANSFORMATION   ORIGINS

We're playing games.
So are you.
24 hours a day.
People's games create the world—
Its ugliness or beauty.
To change the games
Make new ones.
Make games worth playing.
Anywhere, any time, whatever else you're doing,
There are elements of universal games
To practice.
A good game pays off
Whether others play it or not.
So you can change the world now,
Without waiting for others to start.

That's how the Origins sector of the BBS was introduced. The introductory material is explicitly not copyrighted and people are encouraged to download, copy, and pass it around. Here is a sample of the first few introductions that started different lines of discussion in the BBS:

What is Origins?
Let's change the world. The world we have isn't working. Let's create one that does. Let's empower ourselves, independently of governments, corporations, wars, nukes, unemployment, degrading jobs, centralized power, sexism, racism, rampant stupidity, and oppressive laws.
We can organize with our friends for survival, from personal eco-

nomic survival to the prevention of war. We can find a path of integrity, of work worth doing. We can build a movement for human dignity, a community for reconciliation, conflict resolution, and effective social and political action.

How? Origins is both a fellowship and a method for empowerment. We are developing "practices"—forms of training, forms of action, forms of play ritual—that you can use any time, wherever you are, whatever else you are doing. These practices work in our relationships, in our styles of action and our ordinary, everyday moments. They are practices designed to help you now, in your personal and business life; their purpose is to make you stronger as a first step in making the world better. You can learn skills for transforming ugliness into beauty, just as you learn other skills.

Origins works to build practical imagination, competence in being and doing, strength through cooperation and community. Origins combines individual awareness for personal competence and success, with collective awareness to organize community strength against the arms race and other forms of ugliness and degradation.

Origins does not charge money or sell anything. We are not sponsored by or related to any other movement or organization. To remain decentralized, we have no official existence. Instead, this movement is intended to develop as local groups of friends, groups which network with each other as they wish.

Origins is a movement that started on this computer. Origins began on the start-a-religion conference, but we don't call it a religion.

Origins is partly a religion, partly like a Westernized form of yoga society, partly a peace movement. It is a framework for improving your life and improving the world at the same time.

The movement centers on "practices"—actions you can use in everyday life to build effective human relationships, strength of community, and self-awareness. All the practices are based on action. None require any special equipment, settings, leaders, theories, or social status. The human universals of the ordinary, everyday moment, and the personal relationship, form the basis for this training.

Origins has no leaders, no official existence, nothing for sale. Because it started in an open computer conference, no one knows who all the creators are.

We recommend seven practices (Leverage a favor. Ask for help and get it. Use Charisma. Finish a job. Use magic. Observe yourself. Share Grace). But these suggestions are only starters. The idea is to continually develop new training/action methods, as a community project, then discuss and share them through whatever communications media are available. This movement will never be finished, because it seeks a community of permanent innovation.

The irony of my encounter with Origins was the fact that the BBS where I found it folded the week after I downloaded the above-quoted material. I trust that the Origins affinity group found some other place, electronic or otherwise, to evolve their information-age brand of spirituality. Although the majority of BBSs are filled with computer enthusiasts or game players, joke-traders or dirty talkers, the Origins BBS wasn't the only intriguing electronic gathering place I found in my months of online wanderings. And it wasn't the only unusual one. Old communities as well as new ones had discovered a medium for linking together groups of people who might never have known about one another otherwise. Religions, old and new, seemed to be one of the livelier categories of discussion. Christian, Jewish, Moslem, mystic—even neopagan—BBSs seem to be thriving. One of the most startling discoveries I made during my board-browsing expeditions was the pagan faction who announced themselves with the following message:

The Covenant of the Goddess is an umbrella organization for pagan groups of all kinds. It was created in the 60s to provide some structure (and maybe some muscle, since some groups were being harassed by the government) to an otherwise amorphous bunch of covens in Northern California, but eventually had members everywhere. A pagan group mostly refers to witches, although there are

Druid groves and other strictly unallied organizations online as well. Witches means any affinity group which holds as one of its general tenets that Jehovah may not be the guy in charge after all. . . . These definitions are by exclusion because one way of defining the whole pagan movement is as a group that believes in saying yes to more. A coven is an affinity group of witches. The name is very old. Some covens have fierce strict codes of behavior and rules of ceremony and others get together now and then and shoot the shit. By and large, witches have the best parties of any religious group going. There is another organization in the California area known as the New Reformed Orthodox Order of the Golden Dawn, which was started as a gag in the 60s and presently has several thousand members, a good many of which can apparently be counted on to show up for a bash. It is typically pagan, incidentally, to start your largest umbrella organization for a joke. Lots of witches compute, and there are probably a bunch on this very BBS who have not bothered to identify themselves. (Witches have no identifying marks—except that humorous glint in the eye.)

The ARPAnet and networks of BBSs weren't the only place online communities gestated in the early 1980s. Two large companies successfully operated "information utilities" for tens of thousands of people, using banks of mainframe computers to offer relatively high-priced public access to electronic mail and special interest groups (aka SIGs—a techie version of a conference). The advantage to joining the Source or Compuserve is that they are national and very large. And the disadvantage to joining them, besides expense, is that they are national and very large. By the mid-1980s, superminicomputers and third-generation conferencing software, based on refinements of refinements of the first systems created by Turoff and Engelbart, made it possible to create more moderately sized—community sized—conferencing systems.

In 1985, the Point foundation and NETI (Network Technologies, Inc.) founded the Whole Earth Electronic Link, a multi-user conferencing system that is a step grander than a bedroom BBS and a level more local than national information utilities such as Compuserve and Source. The deal got started when the Point Foundation's Stewart Brand, of Whole Earth Catalog reknown, met Dr. Larry Brilliant of NETI at The Western Behavioral Sciences Institute, a think tank that uses computer conferencing to link groups of educators, academics, scientists, and business people. Brand had previously heard of Dr. Brilliant's work with the international medical charity, SEVA, which had used conferencing with admirable success in its battle against blindness in Nepal and other projects. Brilliant told him about the case of the downed copter that made him see computer conferencing as a tool for global social change.

A donated helicopter that was delivering donated medical supplies to a remote Nepalese province had to land with a bad engine. By the time a new engine could be located, funded, shipped, and installed, the medicine would be spoiled. By mobilizing an international network of volunteer experts in aviation, medicine, and international law, Dr. Brilliant and his colleagues were able to locate the nearest replacement part, make contact with officials who could cut international red tape, and find people who were willing to donate the use of aircraft to ship the engine. The success of that venture led Dr. Brilliant to create NETI to spread the use of this community-organizing tool. A new generation of computer conferencing software, PicoSpan, was created. NETI provided the Point foundation with a leased computer and PicoSpan. Point furnished a small office near the Sausalito houseboat colony, the staff, and the Whole Earth constituency. The Well was among the first of a growing number of locally based systems capable of dealing with dozens of users at one time, with a local constituency and national access.

The national access is provided by Usenet, which links the Well to the Worldnet. *Worldnet* is the name that is used to describe the very loose confederation of public, private, and government networks that have become increasingly interconnected with one another. Special gateway computers allow mail to be passed between separate networks, and the use of special software allows individual computers or entire networks to share information. The Usenet is a virtual community consisting of thousands of computers and hundreds of thousands of people. The individual members, which are mostly computer systems at universities or government installations with a sprinkling of public systems like the Well, agree to run a special computer program called Netnews and to automatically call other computers in their local vicinity. The Well, for example, communicates every day with computers at Lucasfilms (where the *Star Wars* movies are made) and at Lawrence Livermore Laboratory (where the real-live thermonuclear Star Wars is designed), and a few other computers in the San Francisco Bay Area.

The computers automatically dial one another and exchange incoming and outgoing mail. Some of the mail consists of entries in a grand, distributed, free-for-all conference, but instead of conferences, the individual entries are clumped in "mailgroups." By exchanging mail with a few close neighbors, who exchange mail with a few other close neighbors, the Usenet enables people to send mail and mailgroups to virtually any site in the world in a matter of days. So each Well member can automatically join the Worldnet by joining a mailgroup and reading and replying. And the Worldnet continues to grow, rather like a virus, as computers call each other and exchange Netnews software.

WHAT GOOD IS A VIRTUAL COMMUNITY?

Virtual communities have several advantages over the old-fashioned communities of place and profession. Because we cannot see one another, we are unable to form prejudices about others before we read what they have to say: Race, gender, age, national origin, and physical appearance are not apparent unless a person wants to make such characteristics public. People whose physical handicaps make it difficult to form new friendships find that virtual communities treat them as they always wanted to be treated—as transmitters of ideas and feeling beings, not carnal vessels with a certain appearance and way of walking and talking (or not walking and not talking). Don't mistake this filtration of appearances for dehumanization: Words on a screen are quite capable of moving one to laughter or tears, of evoking anger or compassion, of creating a community from a collection of strangers.

In traditional kinds of communities, we are accustomed to meeting people, then getting to know them. In virtual communities, you can get to know people and then choose to meet them. In some cases, you can get to know people whom you might never meet on the physical plane. In the traditional community, we search through our pool of neighbors and professional colleagues, of acquaintances and acquaintances of acquaintances, in order to find people who share our values and interests. We then exchange information about one another, share and debate our mutual interests, and sometimes we become friends. In a virtual community we can go directly to the place where our particular interests are being discussed, then get acquainted with those who share our passions. In this sense, the subject of discussion, the idea of affinity that draws a group of individuals together into the discussion, is itself the address: You can't simply pick up a phone and ask to be connected with someone who wants to talk about Islamic art or California wine, or someone with a three-year-old daughter or a thirty-year-old Hudson; you can, however, join a computer conference on any of those topics, then open a public or private correspondence with the previously unknown people you find in that conference. You will find that your chances of making friends are magnified by orders of magnitude over the old methods of finding a peer group.

Because a written, retrievable record exists of all the conversations and exchanges of information that take place, computer-mediated communities have a kind of collective memory. Previous statements can be verified, facts can be found with pointers, and newcomers can find out what all the old hands know simply by studying the record. By coupling this group memory with the use of conferences and messages to find solutions and create consensus, it is possible to augment the intelligence of a group of people, just as computer-based tools like word processors, database systems, and spreadsheets augment the intelligence of individuals. Murray Turoff noted, in 1976:

> I think the ultimate possibility of computerized conferencing is to provide a way for human groups to exercise a "collective intelligence" capability. The computer as a device to allow a human group to exhibit collective intelligence is a rather new concept. In principle, a group, if successful, would exhibit an intelligence higher than any member. Over the next decades, attempts to design computerized conferencing structures that allow a group to treat a particular complex problem with a single collective brain may well promise more benefit for mankind than all the artificial intelligence work to date.[10]

Virtual communities can help their members cope with information overload. The problem with the information age, especially for students and knowledge workers who spend their time immersed in the info-flow, is that there is too much information available and no effective filters for sifting the key data that are useful and interesting to us as individuals. Dreamers in the artificial intelligence research community are trying to evolve "software agents" that can seek and sift, filter and find, and save us from the awful feeling one gets when it turns out that the specific knowledge one needs is buried in fifteen thousand pages of related information. In my virtual community, we don't have software agents (because they don't exist yet), but we do have informal social contracts that allow us to act as software agents for one another. If, in my wanderings through information space, I come across items that don't interest me but which I know one of my group of online friends would appreciate, I send the appropriate friend a pointer to the key datum or discussion. The pointer can direct my friend's attention to a television show, a book, a magazine article, a lecture, an item in a computer conference, and it consists of a very brief description of the information and terse directions on how to gain access to it.

This social contract requires one to give something, and enables one to receive something. I have to keep my friends in mind and send them pointers instead of throwing my informational discards into the virtual scrap heap. It doesn't take a great deal of energy to do that, since I have to sift that information anyway in order to find the knowledge I seek for my own purposes. And with twenty other people who have an eye out for my interests while they explore sectors of the information space that I normally wouldn't frequent, I find that the help I receive far outweighs the energy I expend helping others: A perfect fit of altruism and self-interest. For example, I was invited to join a panel of experts who advise the U.S. Congress Office of Technology Assessment (OTA). The subject of the assessment is "Communication Systems for an Information Age." Before I went to Washington for my first panel meeting, I opened a conference in the Well and invited assorted information freaks, technophiles, and communication experts to help me come up with something to say.

By the time I sat down with the industry representatives, government advisers, regulators, and academic experts at the panel table, I had over two hundred pages of expert advice from my own panel. I wouldn't have been able to garner that much knowledge of my subject in an entire academic or industrial career, and it only took me (and my virtual community) six weeks. The same strategy can be applied to an infinite domain of problem areas, from literary criticism to software evaluation.

Virtual communities have several drawbacks in comparison to face-to-face communication, and these disadvantages must be kept in mind if you are to make use of the advantages of these computer-mediated discussion groups. The filtration factor that prevents one from knowing the race or age of another participant also prevents people from communicating the facial expressions, body language, and tone of voice that constitute the "invisible" but vital component of most face-to-face communications. Irony, sarcasm, compassion, and other subtle but all-important nuances that aren't conveyed in words alone are lost when all you can see of a person is a set of words on a screen. This lack of communication bandwidth can lead to misunderstandings and is one of the reasons that "flames" or heated diatribes that normally wouldn't crop up often in normal discourse seem to appear with relative frequency in computer conferences.

Sociologists point out that schoolchildren and teenagers were not influenced by their peer groups before the widespread adoption of telephone technology, which enabled them to make contact with one another after school hours. Who could have predicted that powerful social side effect of the new communication technology back in the days of the hand-cranked set and party lines? We are in the hand-cranked days of computer mediated communication. One of today's online experiments—an electronic religion, a virtual community, a political network, a form of mental intercourse—will grow into something that will change our lives in unexpected ways.

This atmosphere of experimentation that flourishes today often accompanies the early days of a new communication technology, and only very rarely does it continue when the experiments blossom into big business and mass markets. In the past, most of the enthusiasms of the early adapters eventually were dampened by hard, usually economic, realities. Television was going to become the greatest educational instrument the world has seen. And it has—in ways that nobody predicted and that would appall the early educational enthusiasts. But computer-mediated communication is different from previous technological revolutions in two important ways. First, it is a decentralized technology, in which ordinary citizens can now economically own computing power that only governments could afford twenty-five years ago. A million small computers, linked by ordinary telephone lines, can suddenly wield formidable computing power that is extremely hard to control in a rigidly hierarchical, centralized manner. For better or worse, the ultimate shape of this technology will not be determined by elite groups of capitalists or commissars, but by entire populations.

And the timing of the latest communication revolution, coming as it does at such a pivotal point in history, is important. It appears that the continuing fate of human evolution on this planet is very much in question. A lot of people need all the help they can get to communicate rationally, warmly, and efficiently with a lot of other people, or there might not be any more people at all. It looks as if we might have to invent a whole new kind of community for this planet if we want to continue to exist. Whether or not this can be done is an open question. But there is no question that we are beginning to create the right kind of tools for accomplishing a task of such magnitude and urgency. Sooner or later, if we know what's good for us, we'll use these tools to build a virtual community that numbers in the billions.

NOTES

1. Joseph Campbell, *The Hero with a Thousand Faces* (Princeton: Princeton University Press, 1949), pp. 40–41.
2. Martin Buber, *I and Thou* (New York: Scribners, 1958), p. 7.
3. David Simberloff, book review in *The Sciences*, New York Academy of Sciences, January 1985.
4. E. O. Wilson, *Biophilia* (Cambridge, Mass.: Harvard University Press, 1984).
5. Marc Barasch, "A Hitchiker's Guide to Dreamland," *New Age Journal*, October 1983.
6. Arthur Koestler, *The Act of Creation* (New York: Macmillan, 1964).
7. Ibid.
8. Nikola Tesla, "My Inventions," *Electrical Experimenter*, 1919.
9. Ibid.
10. Roy Amara, John Smith, Murray Turoff, and Jacques Vallee, "Computer Conferencing, a New Medium," *Mosaic*, January–February 1976.

BIBLIOGRAPHY

Amara, Roy, John Smith, Murray Turoff, and Jacques Vallee. "Computer Conferencing, a New Medium." *Mosaic*, January–February 1976.

Arnheim, Rudolf. *Visual Thinking*. Berkeley: University of California Press, 1969.

Barasch, Marc. "A Hitchiker's Guide to Dreamland." *New Age Journal*, October 1983.

Bieliauskas, V. J. *The H-T-P Research Review*, 1965 edition. Los Angeles: Western Psychological Services, 1965.

Buber, Martin. *I and Thou*. New York: Scribners, 1958.

Bush, Vannevar. "As We May Think." *The Atlantic Monthly*, August 1945.

Campbell, Joseph. *The Hero with a Thousand Faces*. Princeton: Princeton University Press, 1949.

Delaney, Gayle. *Living Your Dreams*. New York: Harper and Row, 1979.

Eckholm, Erik. "Why Sex Baffles Biologists." *The New York Times*, April 24, 1986.

Edwards, Betty. *Drawing on the Artist Within, a Guide to Innovation, Invention, Imagination, and Creativity.* New York: Simon & Schuster, 1986.

Faraday, Ann. *Dream Power.* New York: Coward, McCann & Geoghegan, 1972.

Festinger, Leon. "Cognitive Dissonance." *Scientific American,* October, 1962.

Garfield, Patricia. *Creative Dreaming.* New York: Ballantine, 1974.

Holliday, Laurel. *The Violent Sex: Male Psychobiology and the Evolution of Consciousness.* Guerneville, Calif.: Bluestocking Books, 1978.

Jolles, Isaac. *Catalog for the Qualitative Interpretation of the House-Tree-Person.* Los Angeles: Western Psychological Services, 1964.

Koestler, Arthur. *The Act of Creation.* New York: Macmillan, 1964.

LaBerge, Stephen. *Lucid Dreaming.* Los Angeles: Tarcher, 1986.

Lem, Stanislaw. *The Futurological Congress.* New York: Avon, 1974.

Licklider, J.C.R., Robert Taylor, and E. Herbert. "The Computer as a Communication Device." *International Science and Technology,* April 1978.

Miller, George. "The Magical Number Seven, Plus or Minus Two: Some Limits on the Capacity for Processing Information." *Psychology Review,* Vol. 63, No. 2, 1956, pp. 81–97.

Nararane, V. S. *The Elephant and the Lotus.* London: Asia Publishing House, 1965.

O'Flaherty, Wendy Doniger. *Dreams, Illusion and Other Realities.* Chicago: The University of Chicago Press, 1984.

Randhawa, M. S. *The Cult of Trees and Tree Worship in Buddhist-Hindu Sculpture.* New Delhi: All India Fine Arts and Crafts Society, 1964.

Shulman, David, *Tamil Temple Myths.* Princeton: Princeton University Press, 1949.

Simberloff, Daniel. Book review in *The Sciences,* New York Academy of Sciences, January 1985.

Stevenson, Robert L. "A Chapter on Dreams," *The Works of Robert Louis Stevenson,* Vol. 16. London: Chatto and Windus, 1912.

Stewart, Kilton. "Dream Theory in Malayia." In *Altered States of Consciousness,* C. Tart, ed., Garden City, N.Y.: Doubleday, 1972.

Tesla, Nikola. "My Inventions." *Electrical Experimenter,* 1919.

von Franz, Marie-Louise. "The Process of Individuation." In C. G. Jung, *Man and His Symbols,* New York: Doubleday, 1964.

Wilson, E. O. *Biophilia.* Cambridge, Mass.: Harvard University Press, 1984.